# THE MODERN LIBRARY
## OF THE WORLD'S BEST BOOKS

THE COMPLETE GREEK TRAGEDIES

VOLUME II

# AESCHYLUS II

## THE SUPPLIANT MAIDENS
## THE PERSIANS
## SEVEN AGAINST THEBES

*The publisher will be pleased to send, upon request,
an illustrated folder listing each volume in*
THE MODERN LIBRARY

# THE COMPLETE GREEK TRAGEDIES

## VOLUME II

# AESCHYLUS II

## THE SUPPLIANT MAIDENS

## THE PERSIANS

## SEVEN AGAINST THEBES

*Edited by* DAVID GRENE *and* RICHMOND LATTIMORE

THE MODERN LIBRARY    NEW YORK

THE MODERN LIBRARY

is published by

RANDOM HOUSE, INC.

BENNETT CERF • DONALD S. KLOPFER

# CONTENTS

# CONTENTS

THE COMPLETE GREEK TRAGEDIES

VOLUME II

# AESCHYLUS II

THE SUPPLIANT MAIDENS
THE PERSIANS
SEVEN AGAINST THEBES

# THE SUPPLIANT MAIDENS

*Translated and with an Introduction by*

SETH G. BENARDETE

# INTRODUCTION TO
## *THE SUPPLIANT MAIDENS*

It had always been thought by modern scholars that *The Suppliant Maidens* was the earliest Greek play still preserved, and the date of its production was given as *circa* 490 B.C. This opinion was based on stylistic considerations as well as on the fact that the protagonist of the play is the chorus itself, which Aristotle tells us to have been the early condition of the drama. A papyrus recently published, however, would seem to suggest that the trilogy, of which *The Suppliant Maidens* is the first part, was first produced after 470 B.C. Should this prove to be the case, it will be a real puzzle why Aeschylus kept the play in his drawer for twenty years; for it is hardly likely that he should have reverted to the archaism of *The Suppliant Maidens* after having written *The Persians*.

The plot of the play is simple. The fifty daughters of Danaus, descendants of the Argive Io, flee from Egypt to Argos because their Egyptian cousins wish, without their consent, to marry them. They come to a sacred grove near Argos, where the rest of the action takes place. Pelasgus, the King of Argos, is unwilling to grant them sanctuary unless the populace seconds his request; and the populace, convinced by the king and their own father, does grant it. But it is not a moment too soon; for after the maidens hear they are saved, their father informs them that the Egyptian cousins are just landing, and while he goes to bring aid, a herald of their cousins comes to take them away. Pelasgus, however, returns with an armed

3

force, and the herald, threatening war, is forced to withdraw. Then Danaus returns again, counseling them to behave decently, and the play ends with a song of deliverance. Since the second and third parts of the trilogy are lost, and only a few scattered notices of the plot remain, we cannot be certain what Aeschylus' purpose was. In the second play the maidens were somehow forced to marry their cousins (perhaps because Pelasgus dies), but they swear to their father to kill them on their wedding night. All except Hypermnestra fulfil their oath, while she—"splendide mendax," Horace calls her—out of love for her husband saves him. In the last play Hypermnestra is forced to stand trial because she violated her oath; and in a scene reminiscent of that in the *Eumenides*, Aphrodite herself appears and defends her. Part of her speech survives:

> As the sacred heaven longs to pierce the earth,
> So love takes hold of earth to join in marriage,
> And showers, fallen from heaven brought to bed,
> Make the earth pregnant; and she in turn gives birth
> To flocks of sheep and Ceres' nourishment—
> A marriage that drenches the springtime of the woods—
> For all this I am in part responsible.

*The Suppliant Maidens* is an international play. The Danaids are refugees, Greeks by descent, Egyptians in appearance (ll. 234-37, 277-90, 496 ff.), and according to Egyptian law they have no legal right to refuse to marry their cousins. For when Pelasgus wishes to know what right they have, the maidens in reply only declare their hatred of their cousins, implying by their evasion of the question the absence of any legal claim to his protection (ll. 387-91). Thus both by nature and by law they are defenseless. If they really looked like Greeks, as well as were Greeks by an obscure genealogy, and if they had some legal justification, Pelasgus might have been willing to take up their defense without the consent of the people; but once it becomes a case of pure or natural justice independent of all legality, with the maidens' arbitrary dislike of their

4

cousins their only motive, Pelasgus must defer to the will of the people. Since the maidens insist upon the rights of the will alone, Pelasgus allows in turn the people's will to sanction it and make it law. In the second play the oath of the Danaids becomes law, and Hypermnestra, in violating it, repeats her sisters' original defiance of Egyptian law; but as on this occasion it is not a human law that she has betrayed, a goddess must justify her conduct. Aphrodite insists upon the prerogatives of love, a force that transcends even the sacredness of oaths. Thus the trilogy is complete. At first the Egyptians embodied law, though strangely enough lust also supported them, while the Danaids represented a freedom that was not bound by any positive enactments. But once this freedom has been approved by law, Hypermnestra alone remains outside it; and as she cannot be defended merely by a democratic procedure, a universal divine law, more authoritative than even the people's will, must rescue her. Having only the first part of the trilogy, we cannot be confident that Aeschylus' purpose was exactly this; but the claims of the city as opposed to claims still more powerful would seem to underlie the play, claims that at each stage become more contrary to one another and more difficult to resolve.

*The Suppliant Maidens* as a play is not very exciting, and we can easily see why the chorus was later abandoned as the protagonist. A chorus can convey only a lyrical mood; it can hardly support any genuine passion. The Danaids, for example, say they are frightened when the Egyptians are coming, but we do not believe them: their songs, divided into strophe and antistrophe,* betray their detachment, and they always talk more like commentators on their actions than like the actors themselves. Although the choruses of *The Suppliant Maidens* are some of the most beautiful Aeschylus ever wrote, the dialogue seems extremely artificial and forced, with the air of set speeches directed more to the audience than to the

* Throughout this play and *The Persians*, strophes and antistrophes are marked by the symbols — and = respectively.

5

other actors. *The Persians*, on the other hand, suffers from the opposite fault: the speeches, even though long, are dramatic, while the choral songs are far inferior to those of *The Suppliants*. Only in the *Oresteia* did Aeschylus achieve a perfect balance between them.

## CHARACTERS

*Chorus of maidens, daughters of Danaus*
*Danaus, their father*
*Pelasgus, King of Argos*
*Herald of Egyptians, cousins to the Danaans*

# THE SUPPLIANT MAIDENS

SCENE: *A sacred grove near Argos, adorned with statues of Greek gods.*

*Chorus*
    Zeus Protector, protect us with care.
    From the subtle sand of the Nile delta
    Our ship set sail. And we deserted:
    From a holy precinct bordering Syria
    We fled into exile, condemned
    Not for murder by a city's decree,
    But by self-imposèd banishment escaping
    Impious marriage with Egyptus' sons.        10

    Danaus, father, adviser and lord,
    Setting the counters of hope,
    Picked the smallest pawn of grief,
    Quickly to fly through the sea,
    And find anchor at Argos,
    Whence we boast to descend,
    By the breathing caress of Zeus
    On a cow driven wild.

    With suppliant olive branch,
    To what kinder land could we turn?        20

    Whose city, whose earth and bright water,
    Olympian gods, ancient gods below
    Possessing the tomb, and Zeus Savior,

9

Keeper of pious men, receive
(Respectful the air of this land)
These suppliant maidens well.

But that thick swarm of insolent men,                    30
Before ever landing in this swamp waste,
Return them and their ship to the sea;
And by the winter sting of hurricane,
Facing the wild sea, by thunder and lightning,
By rain-winds may they die;
Before appropriating what law protects,
Cousins to lie on unwilling beds.                        40

Now I invoke
The calf of Zeus Avenger
Beyond the sea:
A child from grazing
Cow, genetrix,
Held by the breath of Zeus,
Born with a fateful name:
Epaphus, Caress.—

Him I invoke:
In pastures here our mother
Suffered before:                                         50
I'll show a witness
Faithful but unex-
pected to natives here.
They shall know the truth
At last and at length.=

And if some neighbor here knows bird cries,
Hearing our bitter passion he will think
He hears the hawk-chased, sad bird Metis,                60
The wife of Tereus,—
                        Who weeps with passion
Barred from rivers and the countryside;

Who sang a child's death-dirge, whom she killed,
Perverse her wrath.=

Thus melancholy I
With Ionian songs
Eat my Nile-soft cheek,
My heart unused to tears.                          70
We gather blooms of sorrow,
Anxious if a friend,
Someone, will protect us,
Exiles from a misty land.—

But gods ancestral, hear!
Behold justice kindly.
Truly hating pride
Grant nothing undecreed:                           80
So just you'd be to marriage.
Even war has havens,
Bulwark for the weary
Exile, a respect of gods.=

May his will, if it's Zeus's, be well,
His will not easily traced.
Everywhere it gleams, even in blackness,
With black fortune to man.—

And so certain it falls without slips,             90
By sign of Zeus fulfilled.
Dark are the devices of his counsel,
His ways blind to our sight.=

From towered hopes
He casts men destructive,
No violence
He armors.
All providence
Is effortless: throned,

11

Holy and motionless,
His will is accomplished.—                          100

On mortal pride
Look down, how it waxes
And flourishes
By marriage
Remorselessly:
Intent in its frenzy,
Spur inescapable,
Deceived to destruction.=                           110

I sing suffering, shrieking,
Shrill and sad am weeping,
My life is dirges
And rich in lamentations,
Mine honor weeping.
    I invoke your Apian land,
    You know my foreign tongue.
    Often I tear my Sidonian veils.—               120

We grant gods oblations
Where all is splendid
And death is absent.
O toils undecipherable!
Where lead these billows?
    I invoke your Apian land.
    You know my foreign tongue.
    Often I tear my Sidonian veils.=               130

Linen-bound ship, secure from the sea,
With fair winds brought me;
Nor do I blame.
May Father, timely omniscient,
Perfect a gracious end, that                        140
    Seeds mighty of solemn mother

Escape, O woe,
Unwed, virgin to the bed of man.—

Daughter of Zeus pure, may she behold,
Who guards walls sacred,
Willing my will.
May virgin, rescuing virgins,
In all her power come, that                                    150
   Seeds mighty of solemn mother
   Escape, alas,
   Unwed, virgin to the bed of man.=

But if not,
A sunburnt race
Shall go beseeching
To Zeus of the dead
(Gracious to strangers),
Hanging ourselves,
If Gods Olympian heed not.                                    160
   O Zeus! Sought out by the gods,
   By snake-hate of Io:
   I know Hera's madness
   Conquering all.
   Winter comes by sharp winds.—

Then Zeus in
Injustice hates
His son begotten,
And that is unjust:                                           170
Face now averted
Away from my prayers.
But would that Zeus hearken!
   O Zeus! Sought out by the gods,
   By snake-hate of Io:
   I know Hera's madness
   Conquering all.
   Winter comes by sharp winds.=

*Danaus*

    Prudence, my daughters; prudently you came
    With an agèd father as your trusted pilot.
    And now, with foresight, I advise your taking
    Care to seal my words within your mind.
    I see dust, the silent clarion of arms,              180
    But not in silence are the axles turned;
    Crowds I see, armed with shield and spear,
    Followed by horses and curvèd chariots.
    Perhaps the princes of this land have come
    To meet us, informed by messenger;
    But whether kindly purposed or provoked
    To savageness they speed their armament,
    Here it is best to act the suppliant,
    This rock, this altar of assembled gods,
    Stronger than ramparts, a shield impenetrable.     190
    Now quickly prepare white suppliant wreaths,
    Sign of Zeus sacred, held in the left hand;
    Mournful, respectful, answer needfully
    The strangers; tell distinctly of an exile
    Unstained by murder. Let no boldness
    Come from respectful eye and modest features.
    Not talkative nor a laggard be in speech:       200
    Either would offend them. Remember to yield:
    You are an exile, a needy stranger,
    And rashness never suits the weaker.

*Chorus*

    With prudence, father, you speak to the prudent.
    I shall keep a watch on your discreet commands.
    May Zeus, my ancestor, look on us.

*Danaus*

    May he look then with propitious eye.

*Chorus*

    Now would I wish to be near your side.

*Danaus*
Delay not.

*Chorus*

O Zeus, compassion ere we die.                    210

*Danaus*
If Zeus is willing, this will end well.
And now that bird of Zeus invoke.

*Chorus*
Preserving rays of the sun we call.

*Danaus*
Call on Apollo, the god, who from heaven once fled.

*Chorus*
So knowing this fate, may he have compassion.

*Danaus*
Let him be compassionate, defend us with care.

*Chorus*
What other gods must I invoke?

*Danaus*
                    I see
This trident, a god's symbol.

*Chorus*
                    Who brought us
Here well: may he receive us now well.

*Danaus*
And that is Hermes, by Hellenic custom.            220

15

*Chorus*

    May he be a good herald to those who are free.

*Danaus*

    All gods here at a common altar worship.
    Settle on the sacred ground like doves
    Clustering together, fearing the winged hawks,
    Who hatefully pollute their very blood.
    Bird consumes bird, how could it be pure?
    How, unwilling brides, myself unwilling,
    Could they be pure? Who not even in hell,
    Where another Zeus among the dead (they say)         230
    Works out their final punishment, can flee
    Their guilt of lust. Fix your eye on that
    In answer, that victory be with you well.

            (*Enter the King of Argos and company.*)

*King*

    Whence come these barbarians?
    What shall we call you? So outlandishly
    Arrayed in the barbaric luxury
    Of robes and crowns, and not in Argive fashion
    Nor in Greek? But at this I wonder how         240
    Without a herald, without a guide, without patron,
    You have yet dared to come, without trembling.
    The suppliant olive branch before these gods
    You've placed (it is custom); but Greece no more
    Than that will guess: in other things I could
    Conjecture only, unless your voice will guide.

*Chorus*

    You did not lie about our dress. But to whom
    Do I speak? An Argive citizen, or a herald
    With his sacred staff, or the city's head?

*King*

    Answer me with trust: I am Pelasgus,

Founder of this land, and son of Palaechthon 250
Earth-born. Pelasgians bear my royal name,
And reap the fruits of this earth. I rule the lands
In which the pure Strymon turns, where the sun
Sinks in the west, and limits the Perrhaebi,
Beyond the Pindus, near the Paeoni
And the mountain Dodona: oceans bound my rule:
I lord it over all within that frame.
It is called Apia, after a surgeon 260
Of ancient times, the prophet Apis, son
To Apollo, who from Naupactus once did come,
And cleansed this land of deadly, monstrous
Serpents, that the earth, soaked in old
Curses of blood, had sprung and smeared in wrath.
His remedies and herbs did work a cure
For Argos, and he found a monument
In Argive litanies. There are my testaments. 270
And now you can tell your own ancestry.
We have no patience with long speeches.


*Chorus*

Brief and clear is my tale: Argos we claim
By race, the offspring of a fruitful cow.


*King*

You speak beyond my credence, strangers, claiming
Argive birth: more like Libyans you seem
Than like to women native here; or the Nile may foster 280
Such a likeness; or the images
Of Cyprus, carved by native craftsmen;
And of the camel-backed nomads I've heard,
Neighbors to the Ethiopian;
I should have thought you were the unwed
Barbarous Amazons, were you armed with bows.
But I, instructed, would more exactly know,
How your birth and ancestry is Argive. 290

*Chorus*
>Wasn't Io once in Argos charged
>With Hera's temple?

*King*
>                    Io was, the tale
>Is prevalent.

*Chorus*
>              And wasn't Zeus to a mortal
>Joined?

*King*
>          Which was from Hera unconcealed.

*Chorus*
>How ends these royal jealousies?

*King*
>                              A goddess
>Changed a woman to a cow.

*Chorus*
>                          And Zeus,                    300
>Did he approach the hornèd cow?

*King*
>                          Zeus
>Became a bull, they say.

*Chorus*
>                      How then did Hera answer?

*King*
>She placed on her a guard, all-seeing.

*Chorus*

Who?

*King*
Argos, a son of Earth, whom Hermes slew.

*Chorus*
But what did Hera appoint for ill-omened Io?

*King*
A gnatlike goad it was, or driving sting.

*Chorus*
That the Nile-dwellers call the gadfly.

*King*
That drove her from Argos.

*Chorus*

It confirms my tale.                310

*King*
And so to Canobus and to Memphis she came.

*Chorus*
Where Zeus by touch begot a son.

*King*
Who claims to be the calf of Zeus?

*Chorus*

Epaphus,
Truly named Caress.

*King*

And who from him?

19

*Chorus*
Libya, reaping the greatest name.

*King*
And then?

*Chorus*
Belus of two sons, my father's father.

*King*
Tell me his name.

*Chorus*
Danaus, whose brother      320
Fathered fifty sons.

*King*
Disclose his name
Ungrudgingly.

*Chorus*
Egyptus. Now knowing my ancient
Lineage, might you succor an Argive band.

*King*
You seem to share of old this land: but how
Did you bring yourself to leave your father's
Home? What fortune did swoop upon you?

*Chorus*
Lord Pelasgus, shifting are the ills of men.
Nowhere is trouble seen of the same wing.
Who wished for this unexpected flight,
To land at Argos, formerly natives here,      330
Cowering in hate of the marriage bed?

*King*
Why have you come to these assembled gods?

Why do you hold the fresh white olive branch?

*Chorus*
To be no household-slave to Egyptus' sons.

*King*
By hatred or by law? . . .

*Chorus*
                              Who buys a master
From kin? . . .

*King*
                    So greater grows the strength of mortals.

*Chorus*
To desert those distressed is easy.

*King*
                              How
With piety could I act?

*Chorus*
                         Deny the demand                340
Of Egyptus' sons.

*King*
                    But hard's *your* demand to wage
A new war.

*Chorus*
               But justice protects her allies.

*King*
If only she shared from the start.

*Chorus*
Respect the ship of state thus crowned.

**King**

    I shudder before these shaded altars.

**Chorus**

    Yet hard is the wrath of Zeus the protector.
    Son of Palaechthon,
    Listen to me with a caring heart,
    Lord of Pelasgians.
    Protector, behold an exile surrounded:
    A calf, wolf-pursued, on steep rocks,           350
    Confides in the herdsman's strength,
    And bleats her pains.—

**King**

    I see this crowd of gods assenting, each
    Shadowed by the fresh-cut olive branch.
    Yet may this friendship conceal no doom,
    Nor strife for us arise in unexpected
    And unpremeditated ways.

**Chorus**

    Daughter of Zeus,
    Master of lots, may behold a flight          360
    Innocent, Themis!
    And thou from the younger, ancient in wisdom,
    Learn, . . .
    Respecting the suppliant,
    A holy man.=

**King**

    You are not suppliants at my own hearth.
    If the city stains the commonweal,
    In common let the people work a cure.
    But I would make no promises until
    I share with all the citizens.

**Chorus**

    You are, yes, the city, the people,          370

A prince is not judged.
The land, the hearth, the altar you rule
With the single vote and scepter;
Enthroned you command,
And fill every need.
Of pollution be watchful.—

King

Pollution on my enemies! Without
Harm I cannot aid you; nor is it sensible
To despise these your earnest prayers.
I am at a loss, and fearful is my heart,
To act or not to act and choose success.                380

Chorus

Regard him, above, the protector,
A watchdog of men
Distressed who sit at neighboring hearths,
But obtain no lawful justice.
Yet anger of Zeus
The Suppliant remains,
Who is charmed by no pity.=

King

If Egyptus' sons rule you by customs
Native to your city, claiming nearest
Of kin, who would wish in that to oppose them?
According to laws at home you must plead,          390
How over you they lack authority.

Chorus

Yet subject to men would I never be!
I plot a course under the stars,
Escape from a heartless marriage.
Take as an ally justice.
Choose the side of the gods.—

*King*

    The choice is not easy: choose me not as judge.
    I said before that never would I act
    Alone, apart from the people, though I am ruler;
    So never may people say, if evil comes,           400
    "Respecting aliens the city you destroyed."

*Chorus*

    Both sides of related blood he sees,
    Zeus holds a sensitive balance,
    To evil and the righteous weighing
    Just and unjust fairly.
    Why fear to act justly?=

*King*

    We need profound, preserving care, that plunges
    Like a diver deep in troubled seas,
    Keen and unblurred his eye, to make the end
    Without disaster for us and for the city;         410
    That neither strife may bring reprisals, nor,
    If we should give you back, seated thus
    On seats of gods, we settle the god, destructive
    Alastor, in this land, who even in Hades
    Never frees the dead. Seem we not
    To need preserving counsel?

*Chorus*

    Take care and be,
    Justly, the pious protector,
    Exile betray not,           420
    Exile pursued by,
    Cast out by, the godless.—

    See me not seized,
    From seat of gods to be seized,
    O lord with full power.

Know the pride of men,
Beware of god's anger.=

Bear not to see
A suppliant by force                                    430
Led from these statues,
Seized by my garments,
Like a horse by the bridle.—

Do what you will,
Thy house remains to pay,
Fined in thy children:
Justice is equal.
Mark the justice of Zeus.=

*King*
    I have pondered, and here I'm run aground:
    'Gainst you or them necessity is strained        440
    For mighty war, as fastly drawn as ships
    Held by the windlass: yet anchorage is never
    Free from pain. When wealth is sacked and homes
    Are pillaged, Zeus yet another fortune may bestow;
    Or when the tongue has failed, a healing word
    May spread a counter-balm: but if consanguine
    Blood is to stay unshed, we must sacrifice
    To slaughter many kine to many gods,             450
    A cure of grief. I am spent by this dispute:
    I wish an ignorance more than art of ill:
    Against my judgment may it turn out well.

*Chorus*
    But hear the end of my reverent prayers.

*King*
    Well?

*Chorus*
        Clasps and belts and bands I have.

*King*
  They are doubtless proper for women.

*Chorus*
                    Here, you know,
  Are fine devices.

*King*
              Tell me.                                    460

*Chorus*
                  Unless you promise—

*King*
  What would your bands accomplish?

*Chorus*
  Statues with new tablets to adorn.

*King*
                      Speak simply.

*Chorus*
  From these gods to hang.

*King*
                  A whip to the heart.

*Chorus*
  Now you understand, for eyes I gave you.

*King*
  Alas! everywhere I'm gripped in strange holds,
  And like a swollen river evils flood:
  Embarked on a sea of doom, uncrossed, abysmal,    470
  Nowhere is anchorage. If I leave

26

This debt unpaid, you've warned of pollution
That shall strike unerringly; but if
I stand before these walls, and bring the battle
To the very end against Egyptus'
Sons, wouldn't that become a bitter waste—
Men to bleed the earth for women's sake?
But yet the wrath of Zeus the Suppliant—
The height of mortal fear—must be respected.
Now then, agèd father of these maidens,⠀⠀⠀⠀⠀⠀⠀480
Gather those wreaths in your arms; and at other
Altars of the native gods replace them:
Then no one of the native people, who delight
In blame, by seeing proof of your arrival,
Could reproach me; and pity they may feel
For you, and hate those men's arrogance.
May the people be gracious! Everyone,
To those weaker than themselves, is kind.

*Danaus*

To have found a stranger, reverent and kind,⠀⠀⠀⠀490
We highly prize. And now, let native guides,
To grant me safety as I go, escort me
To the temple altars: nature made
My shape unlike to yours, even as the Nile
And the Inachus bear no resemblance
In their nurture. Beware lest rashness burgeon
Into fear: ignorance has often killed
A friend.

*King*

⠀⠀⠀⠀⠀Attend: the stranger speaks well.⠀⠀⠀⠀500
Guide him to the civil altars, the seats
Of gods; and say no more than this to whom
You meet: "To the gods' hearth we bring a sailor."

⠀⠀⠀⠀⠀⠀⠀⠀⠀(*Exit Danaus, attended.*)

27

**Chorus**

> Him you instructed, and he is gone; but I,
> How shall I act? What sign of confidence
> Is yours to give me?

**King**

>                         Leave your wreaths here,
> A sign of grief.

**Chorus**

>                         And here I leave them by your
> Command.

**King**

>             Toward that grove now turn.

**Chorus**

>                                             But how
> Would a public grove protect me?

**King**

>                             Never                    510
> To rape of birds shall we expose you.

**Chorus**

> But to them more hateful than heartless snakes?

**King**

> Propitiated, speak auspiciously.

**Chorus**

> You know how fear does fret impatiently?

**King**

> Excessive fear is always powerless.

**Chorus**

> Soothe then my heart in word and deed.

*King*

    Your father will not long desert you; and I,
    Assembling all the native people, shall
    Make the commons well disposed, and teach
    Your father all that he must say.
    Now remain here, and beseech the native        520
    Gods with your prayers to bring what you desire.
    I shall go arranging all: may Persuasion
    And Fortune attend me!

                           *(Exit King.)*

*Chorus*

    Lord of Lords most bless'd,
    Most perfect strength of bless'd,
    Happy Zeus obey
    And let it be:
    Remove the pride of men,
    Pride well hated;
    And cast in a purpled sea
    The black-benched doom.—        530

    Look upon our race
    Ancient of ancestor loved,
    Change to a happy tale
    Favoring us:
    Remember many things,
    You touched Io.
    We claim a descent from Zeus,
    And birth from this land.=

    To my mother's ancient track I turned,
    In a rich pasture eating flowers
    She was seen, whence Io        540
    By gadfly raged
    Distraught escaped;
    Passing many races,

Cutting in two the land,
The raging strait defined;—
Through lands of Asia fast she went,
And across Phrygia grazing sheep;
And the city of Teuthras passing,
And Lydian vales,                                    550
Cilician hills,
Race Pamphylian hurried
Through ever-flowing streams,
And land of Aphrodite.=

She came by dart distressed
Of a cowherd winged
To rich groves of Zeus,
A pasture fed by snow and attacked
By Typhon's rage,                                    560
The Nile-waters by disease untouched;
Herself crazed,
With grief, stinging pains,
Bacchant of Hera.—

And men who then lived there
At her strangeness trembled,
With pale fear at heart,
Beheld a creature vexed, half-breed,
In part a cow,
And woman in turn, a monster marveled at.           570
Who then charmed
The wretch wandering-far
Furious Io?=

Of endless sovereignty
Lord Zeus charmed,
By strength gentle of Zeus
And divine breaths
Was she cured, weeping
Her grievous shame,

Bearing the burden of Zeus,                                580
Told without falsehood,
She bore a blameless child,—

Through great time bless'd;
All earth shouts,
"Of Zeus fruitful in truth
This race: who else
Would cure her of sly
Dieases of Hera?"
There is the working of Zeus,
Here is Epaphus' race:
Of both the truth is spoken.=

Whom beside him                                            590
More justly would I call?
Father our gardener, worker, and lord,
A craftsman ag'd in wisdom,
Propitious the wind is of Zeus.—

Stronger none rule,
Beneath no one enthroned,
Seated above he respects none below.
His deeds are quick as words,
He hastens what counsel decrees.=

(*Enter Danaus.*)

*Danaus*
    Take heart, my children, well are cast the people's    600
    Final vote.

*Chorus*
            O hail, my envoy, my dearest
    Herald. Tell us what end's been authorized?
    And where the populace, by show of hands,
    Has thrown its weight.

*Danaus*

>                    The Argives have decreed
> Not doubtfully, so as to change my aging
> Heart to youth again; so bristled thick
> The air with hands, resolving thus the law:
> Free we are to settle here, subject
> Neither to seizure nor reprisal, claimed          610
> Neither by citizen nor foreigner.
> But if they turn to force, whoever rich
> In lands refuses succor, shall be stripped
> Of offices and banished publicly.
> The king persuaded, prophesying Zeus
> The Suppliant would fatten rich his wrath
> To feed insatiate suffering,
> And show itself as twin defilements,          620
> In and outside the city. Hearing this,
> The Argives, not even summoned, voted all.
> They heard, and easily were convinced by supple
> Rhetoric; but Zeus still crowned the end.

*Chorus*

> Come then, let us offer
> For the Argives good prayers,
> A return for good things.
> And may Zeus Stranger behold
> From the mouth of a stranger
> Offerings in true frankness,
> A perfect end for all things.
>
> And now Zeus-born gods          630
> Might you hear our prayers,
> When libations we pour:
> Never slain by fire
> This Pelasgian land,
> Never wanton War
> Found a danceless cry,
> Harvesting mortals

In a changed harvest;
 For compassion they showed us,
 And voted with kindness,      640
 Respecting Zeus's suppliants,
 This wretched flock of sheep.—

Nor cast they their votes
On the side of men
By dishonoring us;
Watching Zeus Avenger
(Like a spy he sees)
Who is hard to fight:
Who desires his home
Stained in its rafters?      650
For he heavily presses.
 The suppliants of Zeus sacred,
 Related blood, they respected.
 Then to gods shall they be pleasing
 With altars scoured clean.=

So out of shadowed lips let fly
Honorable prayers:
Never a plague
Empty the city,      660
Strife never bleed
With native dead the land.
 Flower of youth may it ripen unplucked,
 And partner of Aphrodite, War,
 May he cut not their bloom.—

And laden altars, welcoming,
Set them ablaze.
Well would be ruled
Cities respecting      670
Zeus above all,
Who guides by ancient law.
 Other protectors we pray to be born

33

For always, and Hecate-Artemis
Birth by women protect.=


Let no murderous plague
Come upon the city destroying,                                    680
Without the dance, without lute
Father of tears Ares arming,
And the intestine war's shout.
    May the bitter swarms of ill
    Far from the people sit;
    May the Lycian Apollo
    To all the youth be kind.—


And may Zeus to perfection
Bring the fruit of each season;                                   690
And many young in the fields
Pasturing cattle beget:
May they obtain from gods all.
    May the pious songs be sung
    At altars by minstrels;
    May the lyre-loving voices
    From holy lips arise.=


May the people who strengthen the city
Protect its dignity well;
Whose rule's providential in common counsel;                      700
And before arming Ares,
To strangers without grief
May they grant justice.—


May the gods who possess the city
Be honored by citizens well
With sacrificial laurel, ancestral.
For respect of one's parents
Is third among laws
Written by Justice.=

*Danaus*

Thank you, dear children, for these modest prayers;    710
But from your father tremble not to hear
New intelligence. From this outpost,
Protector of suppliants, I spy that ship;
Clearly it shows; nor do I fail to mark
How its sails are trimmed and sides made fast,
And how her bow does seek the way with painted
Eye; and the ship, obedient, hears all too well
Her tiller's governance. And the men on board
I see, black in limb, their clothes white linen.
All the other ships and allied force    720
I see; but under land the lead, its sail
Now furling, rows with timed beat. And you
Must, quietly and temperately facing
The event, ignore none of these gods.
And I, with advocates, shall come. Perhaps
An envoy or a herald comes, desiring
To lead you away as reprisals.
But nothing shall happen. Never fear him.
Still it is better, if we are slow,    730
That refuge to remember. Take heart.
Surely in time the day shall come when all
Who had dishonored the gods shall pay.

*Chorus*

Father, I fear, as swift ships come;
No length of time does stand between us.
   Terror has me, excessive fear,
   If flights of wandering profit not.
   Father, I am spent by fear.—

*Danaus*

As final was the Argive vote, my daughters,
Take heart: they shall fight for you, I know.    740

*Chorus*

Mad is the race Egyptian, cursed,

35

In war unsated: I speak what you know.
  Dark ships they have, and strongly built;
  They sailed and so succeed in anger
  With an army large and dark.=

*Danaus*

  But here many shall they find, whose limbs
  The sun's made lean in noonday heat.

*Chorus*

  Leave us not behind, alone, father! I pray.
  Women are nothing alone; no Ares is in them.
    Deadly purposed and crafty minds                    750
    With impure hearts, just as ravens,
    They heed no altar.—

*Danaus*

  Well that would aid us, my daughters,
  If to the gods, as to you, they are hateful.

*Chorus*

  They feared not these tridents, no awe of gods;
  Their hands they shall not keep from me, father.
    Arrogant with unholy rage,
    Gluttonous, dog-hearted, obeying
    In nothing the gods.=

*Danaus*

  A fable tells that wolves possess more strength        760
  Than dogs, and reeds cannot conquer wheat.

*Chorus*

  We must guard ourselves against the rage
  Of wanton men, monstrous and profane.

*Danaus*

  The reefing of a sail is never swift,

Nor is the anchoring, with ropes to be secured;
And even safe at anchorage the helmsman
Lacks courage, and mostly when come to harborless
Shores, and the sun has sneaked away to night,
It breeds in prudent pilots pain as sharp                    770
As birth itself; nor would a host find landing
Easy, before each ship takes courage in
Her moorings. But you, fearful at heart, take heed
Of the gods, while I, bringing aid, shall return
To defend you: an agèd messenger the city
Cannot blame, youthful in eloquence.

(*Exit Danaus.*)

*Chorus*

O mountainous land, justly respected,
What shall befall us? Where shall we flee,
If in Apian lands some dark abyss somewhere?
Black smoke might I be
Bordering clouds of Zeus;                                    780
Invisible completely
As unseen dust might I die.—

My heart without fright would no longer be;
Darkness flutters in my heart.
I am seized by his warnings: I am spent by fear.
And willing would I be
Fated to die hanging,
Before that man should touch me:                            790
May Hades rule me before!=

Where might there be a throne of air?
Against it wet clouds become snow?
Or smooth, steep, lonely,
Overhanging, distant,
Vulture-haunted rocks,
Witnessing my fall,

Before by force meet
A heart-rending marriage? —

Prey then for dogs and native birds,                    800
A feast I shall not refuse them.
For death grants freedom
From lámentable ills.
Let that fate before
My marriage-bed come.
But where is still means
To free us from marriage? =

Shriek and shout a cry to heaven,
Perfect prayers to the gods,
To me relief and fulfilment;                            810
And Father, seeing the battle,
Behold with just eyes
Violence unkindly.
Respect your suppliants,
Protector, omnipotent Zeus! —

Proud and heartless Egyptians—
Men pursuing an exile,
Intent on capturing me,
With shouts many and wanton.                            820
But you completely,
Zeus, hold the beam of
The balance. What without you
Is brought to completion for men? =

(*Enter Herald of Egyptians, attended.*)
Cry! O woe! Alas!
Here, this ravisher from the ship!
Before that, ravisher, would you die!
I see this beginning of my woes.                        830
Alas! O woe! Escape!
Stern-hearted in insolence,

Hard to bear on land, at sea,
Lord of the land, protect us!

*Herald*
    Hurry!
    Hasten to the boats
    Fast as you are able.
    Lest torn and pricked,
    Pricked and scratched you'll be,
    Bloody and bloodstained,                          840
    Your heads cut off!
    Hurry, hasten, curses! curses! to the boats!

*Chorus*
    On the flowing salt-path
    With your masterful pride
    With your bolted ship
    Would you had died!

*Herald*                                              850
    Cease your cries. Leave your seats.
    Go to the ships. You without honor,
    You without city, I cannot respect.—

*Chorus*
    Never fruitful water
    Might I see again, whence
    Grows the living root—
    Murder!—and blooms.

*Herald*
    I shall lead—I am brave—
    Down to the ship, up on the ladder.             860
    Willing, unwilling, you shall go.=

*Chorus*
    Oh, alas, woe.

Oh, would that you had helpless died
By the sea-washed grove
Wandering at Sarpedon's tomb,
Piled up with sand                                              870
Among wet breezes.


*Herald*

Shriek and shout and call the gods.
You shall not jump the Egyptian ship.
Bewail and shout and mourn with sorrow.—


*Chorus*

Oh, alas, woe.
Outrage! when you howl off-shore,
With your boasts overflow;
Whom the great Nile might behold
Raging in your pride,                                           880
And drown your violence.


*Herald*

Board the swift boat at once!
Let no one falter: I'll have no awe
Of precious curls when I shall drag you.=


*Chorus*

Alas, father, to the sea he leads me;
Like a spider, step by step,
A dream, a black dream,
Cry, O woe, cry!
Earth, Mother Earth,                                            890
Avert his fearful cry.
O son, son of Earth, O Zeus.


*Herald*

I do not fear these gods before me: they
Did not nurse me, their nursing did not age me.—

*Chorus*

A two-footed serpent quivers near,
Like a viper, bites my foot,
A poisonous thing.
Cry, O woe, cry!
Earth, Mother Earth,
Avert his fearful cry.                                    900
O son, son of Earth, O Zeus.

*Herald*

Your finery I shall not pity, if
None will go to the ship resignedly.=

*Chorus*

We perish, lord, we suffer pain!

*Herald*

O many lords, Egyptus' sons, you soon
Will see—take heart!— and blame no anarchy!

*Chorus*

O first commanders, undone am I!

*Herald*

Methinks I shall resort to dragging you:
My words you clearly have not listened to.            910

(*Enter the King, attended.*)

*King*

You there! What is done? By what insolence
Dare you insult this land of Pelasgian men?
Think you you have come to a woman's land? You are
Barbarians, and you trifle insolently
With Greeks, and, off the mark in everything,
In nothing upright stand.

41

*Herald*

How did I err?
What do I do without justice?

*King*

You know
Not how to be a stranger.

*Herald*

Though finding what I lost?

*King*
To what patron did you speak?

*Herald*

To Hermes the Searcher,   920
The greatest patron.

*King*

You speak of gods but have
No reverence.

*Herald*

The Nile deities I revere.

*King*
And these gods are nothing?

*Herald*

I'll lead them away,
If no one prevents me.

*King*

You shall regret it,
If you touch them.

*Herald*

You speak unkindly to strangers.

*King*

    The thieves of gods I shall not befriend.

*Herald*

    I shall tell Egyptus' sons.

*King*

    What's that to me that I should yield my flock?

*Herald*

    But if I knew, more clearly could I tell—       930
    A herald should report exactly each
    Particular. What shall I say? And who
    Does rob me of these cousins? Yet war does give
    Its verdict without witnesses, nor in silver's
    Grip does it quit its suit, before many
    Are thrown and kick off life.

*King*

                     Why must you tell a name?
    In time you and your companions will know;
    Though, were these willing, with good will of heart,
    You could lead them away, if pious speech      940
    Persuaded them: thus unanimous the vote
    Decreed, never to surrender them to force.
    Joined, doweled, and bolted stays this law,
    That neither scratched on tablets, nor book-sealed,
    You hear announced by the tongue of freedom's voice.
    Now get out of my sight!

*Herald*

                  We seem to wage new wars.    950
    May victory and conquest fall to men!

*King*

    And men is what you'll find here, who don't
    Guzzle a brew of barley-beer!

                         (*Exit Herald.*)

Now all of you, attended by your maids,
Take heart and go to the well-protected city,
Locked by towers in dense array. And many
Homes there are of public property, and I
Am also housed with a lavish hand; there you may
With many others live; or if it pleases                    960
More, you may live alone. Of these the best
And most agreeable choose. Myself and all
The citizens protect you, whose voted will
Is now fulfilled. Why wait for those with more
Authority?

**Chorus**

In return for good things,
May good things teem,
Best of Pelasgians!
Kindly escort my father here,
Danaus, prudent, brave and wise.                           970
His is the counsel where to dwell,
Kindly disposed the place with good
Fame and repute among the people:
Everyone's quick to blame the alien.
May it be for the best!

*(Exit King. Enter Danaus, attended.)*

**Danaus**

My children, to Argives it is meet to pour               980
Libations, pray and sacrifice as to gods
Olympian, who unhesitant preserved us.
What had been done, for native friends kindly,
Bitterly against your cousins, they heard;
And gave these armed attendants as a meed
Of honor, that no spear-wielded fate be mine
In dying, lest I burden on the land
An ever-living grief. You must be grateful
Even more than I for what I have obtained.                 990

44

Above my other counsels cut this wisdom:
Time becomes the touchstone of the alien,
Who bears the brunt of every evil tongue.
The easy targe of calumny. I beg
You not to bring me shame, you who have
That bloom which draws men's eyes: there is no simple
Guard for fruit most delicate, that beasts
And men, both winged and footed, ravage:                    1000
So Venus heralds harvests lush with love;
And all, at the sleek comeliness of maidens,
Do shoot enchanted arrows from their eyes,
Overcome by desire. Let no shame for us,
But pleasure for our enemies, be done,
For which, in great toil, great seas were ploughed.
We have the choice (mere luck) of living either
With Pelasgus, or at the city's cost.                       1010
Only regard this command of your father:
Honor modesty more than your life.

*Chorus*

All else may gods Olympian bless; but, father,
Be not anxious for our summer's blush,
For, lest the gods deliberate anew,
We'll hold to the course our past intent has set.

*Chorus A (of maidens)*

Come now to the city,
Praising blessèd lord gods,
Who shelter the city
And about the Erasinus dwell.                               1020
Take up and accompany,
Servants, the song, and praise
For the city, no longer the Nile,
Respect with your psalms,—

But streams, that with quiet
Through the land fulness pour,

45

And gladden this earth with
Waters brilliant and rich.                                    1030
May Artemis sacred see,
Pitying us: by force
Of Aphrodite no marriage come,
A prize for the hated.=

Chorus B (of servants)
    But careless not of Cypris this gracious song:
    With power equal to Hera nearest to Zeus,
    Honored the goddess sly-intent
    In rites sacred and solemn;
    Which share with a fond mother
    Desire and, to whom no denial,                            1040
    Persuasion; and Aphrodite
    A province to Concord bestowed,
    And Eros whispering wanton.—

    But bitter winds, and harsh and evil grief,
    And battles bloody and deadly I fear before.
    How did they sail so easily
    In swift-winged pursuit?
    Whatever is doomed becomes.
    Infinite the mind is of Zeus,
    Who cannot be bypassed.                                   1050
    To many a woman before
    Has marriage come as an ending.=

Chorus A
    May great Zeus ward off
    An Egyptian marriage for me.

Chorus B
    That would be best.

Chorus A
    Would you charm the intractable?

46

*Chorus B*
But the future you know not.—

*Chorus A*
But Zeus's mind profound,
How am I to plumb?

*Chorus B*
Pray for the mean.                                        1060

*Chorus A*
What limit do you teach me now?

*Chorus B*
Ask the gods nothing excessive.=

*Chorus*
Lord Zeus may he deprive us
Of an ill marriage
And a bad husband,
As Io was released from ill,
Protected by a healing hand,
Kind might did cure her.—

And strength may he assign us.
I am content if ill                                        1070
Is one-third my lot,
And justly, with my prayers,
Beside the saving arts of god,
To follow justice.=

(*Exit all.*)

47

# THE PERSIANS

*Translated and with an Introduction by*

SETH G. BENARDETE

# INTRODUCTION TO
## *THE PERSIANS*

*The Persians* was produced at Athens in 472 B.C., eight years after the naval battle at Salamis, which the play celebrates. We learn from its Argument that it was modeled on a lost play, *The Phoenissae* of Phrynichus, but that Phrynichus had announced at once the defeat of Xerxes, whereas Aeschylus presents a chorus of old men who voice their hopes and fears, by themselves and with Xerxes' mother, before the news of the defeat comes. This delay of course makes the Persians' defeat so much the greater, as it heightens the magnificence of their doom. The Queen then invokes her dead husband Darius (at whose tomb the scene is laid), who had led an unsuccessful expedition against Greece ten years before. He consoles the Queen and Chorus but predicts another disaster at Plataea (479 B.C.). Soon afterward, Xerxes, his garments torn, returns alone, and he and the Chorus conclude the play with a lament.

*The Persians* is unique in several ways. It is the only extant Greek tragedy that is not mythical but based on a contemporary event. The daring of such a presentation is easy to imagine. To show sympathetically, *sine ira et studio*, on the stage at Athens the defeat of her deadliest enemy testifies to the humanity of Aeschylus and the Athenians. No other tragedian we know of, of any country at any time, has ever dared to go so far in sympathizing with his country's foe. It is the more remarkable when we consider that Aeschylus himself and almost all of his audience fought at Salamis or Plataea and that the war, moreover, was between freedom and slavery. Here are the Persians, having started an unjust war and suffering a deserved defeat, presented not as criminals but rather as great and noble, dying deaths that are to be as much pitied as the deaths of Athenians. To praise the Athenians at Athens, Socrates remarks, or the Spartans at Sparta is not very difficult; but to praise the Athenians at Sparta or the Spartans at Athens demands great rhetorical skill; and for Aeschylus to praise before their conquerors the Persians, the enemies of all Greece, is without precedent and without imitation.

Although *The Persians* is historical in substance, Aeschylus deliberately introduced what the entire audience must have known to be false. He makes up Persian names, very few of which correspond to the generals we know to have been at the battle; his figures for the size of Xerxes' fleet at Salamis are greatly exaggerated; the Persians call upon Greek gods, though everyone knew that their gods were different; the Queen performs a Greek sacrifice at the tomb of Darius; neither the Chorus (except once) nor Darius mentions the Persians' defeat at Marathon only ten years before; and perhaps what is most striking, Aeschylus invokes from the past Darius, so that his presence, being both ghostly and real, might transform an ugly reality into a poetic past. By thus changing many details of the real story, Aeschylus removes the Persian War to the realm of myth, where the memory of his audience is prevented from confirming or denying at every point the truth of what he says.

The contemporary is almost perforce untragic, for excessive attention to detail (and the contemporary must be shown accurately) stifles poetry and does not allow the poet to alter his subject; whereas tragedy, being abstracted from the present, is given a free rein, unhampered by what the audience knows to be so, to mold the story to its own demands. Just as verse is an abstraction from prose, reducing it to order, so tragedy abstracts from history and brings necessity out of chance.

If Aeschylus addressed his play specifically to his Athenian countrymen, how can he also speak to us, who are not Athenians, across the reach of time? This certainly must be said. The Persian War was not merely one parochial war among others, in which the issues of right and wrong are ambiguous, as was the case in the Peloponnesian War. The Persian War was a war of liberty versus despotism, and all free men of all times in reading *The Persians* will identify their cause with the cause of the Greeks. In this sense, then, we are Athenians ourselves, and thus our sympathies and understanding become sufficiently enlarged to comprehend the merits of our foes.

Since the doom of the Persians is impressed upon us by the regular meters of the chorus, which convey even to our ears the effect of marching or lament, I have tried, so far as English would allow, to reproduce them in such a way that the reader can "hear" the mood of each song. I hope that, after a little practice on his part, the rhythm will become clear.

## CHARACTERS

*Chorus of Persian elders*
*Queen of Persia, wife of Darius,*
   *mother of Xerxes*
*Persian Herald*
*Ghost of Darius*
*Xerxes*

# THE PERSIANS

SCENE: *In the background the palace of Xerxes at Sousa, in the center foreground the tomb of Darius.*

*Chorus*
    Of the Persians gone
    To the land of Greece
    Here are the trusted:
    As protectors of treasure
    And of golden thrones
    We were chosen by Xerxes—
    Emperor and king,
    Son of Darius—
    In accord with age
    Guards of the country.

    For the king's return
    With his troops of gold
    Doom is the omen          10
    In my heart convulsed,
    As it whines for its master;
    For all Asia is gone:
    To the city of Persians
    Neither a herald nor horseman returns.

    And some Agbatana
    And some Sousa and
    Ancient Kissa leaving,
    Both on horse and on ship

And on foot displayed
Legions of battle: 20
Artaphrenes, Megabates,
Astaspes, Amistres,
Leaders of Persians, kings,
Who are slaves of the greatest of kings,
Guarding the legions they rush,
And as bowman and knight,
With their temper resolved,
Fearful in aspect,
Dreadful in battle.

And exultant in horses
Artembares, Masistres, 30
The brave archer Imaeus,
And Pharandakas,
And the driver of horses
Sousthenes.

And others were sent
By the flourishing Nile:
Egyptian-born Sousiscanes,
Pegastagon, great Arsames
Ruler of sacred Memphis;
And Ariomardus
Governing ancient Thebes;
And who dwelling by marshes
Are rowers of ships,
Skilful and countless. 40

And the Lydians soft
Who inhabit the coast
Follow commanders and kings:
Metrogathes and brave Arkteus,
And golden Sardis send
Many charioteers,

Horses by threes and by fours,
Fearful the sight to behold.

And the neighbors of Tmolus—
They threaten to yoke
In servitude Hellas;                                    50
And the Mysian lancers,
Tharybis, Mardon,
Anvils of battle.
And golden Babylon
Pours forth her crowds—
Borne by their ships—
Who in drawing the bow
Rely on their boldness.
And the tribes from all Asia
Who carry the sword
Follow beneath the
Awesome parade of their king.

Thus of the Persian land
Of her men the flower is gone,
Nursed by the earth, and all Asia                      60
Laments, consumed by desire;
And parents and wives
Counting the days
Tremble at lengthening time.

The destroyer of cities now,
That kingly army, has gone
Over the strait to the land
On linen-bound pontoons—
Tightly was clamped the way—
Helle of Athamas crossing,                             70
Yoking the neck of the sea.—

And the furious leader the herd
Of populous Asia he drives,

Wonderful over the earth,
And admirals stern and rough
Marshals of men he trusts:
Gold his descent from Perseus,
He is the equal of god.=                          80

In his eyes lazuli flashing
Like a snake's murderous glances,
With his mariners, warriors, many,
And his Syrian chariot driving,
Hard on the glorious spearmen
The archer Ares he leads.—

To the great torrent of heroes
There is none worthily equal,
Who resist, by defenses securèd,
The unconquerable billows of ocean:          90
Persians are never defeated,
The people tempered and brave.=

For divine fate has prevailed since            102
It enjoined Persians to wage wars,
Which destroy towers and ramparts,
And the glad tumult of horsemen,
And cities overthrown.—

When the vast ocean was foaming,
By the winds boisterous whitened,
Then they learned, trusting to cables
And to pontoons which convey men,
To scan the sacred sea.=                        113

  Deceitful deception of god—                   93
  What mortal man shall avoid it?
  With nimbleness, deftness, and speed,
  Whose leaping foot shall escape it?
  Benign and coaxing at first

It leads us astray into nets which
No mortal is able to slip,
Whose doom we never can flee.                    101

Thus sable-clad my heart is torn,
Fearful for those Persian arms,
Lest the city hear, alas!
That reft of men is Sousa;—

And lest the city Kissa shall,
When the crowds of women cry,
Sing antiphonal, alas!                           120
And rend their garb of mourning.=

All the horse and infantry
Like a swarm of bees have gone
With the captain of the host,
Who joined the headlands of either land,
Crossing the yoke of the sea.—                   130

Beds with longing fill with tears,
Persian wives in softness weep;
Each her armèd furious lord
Dismissed with gentle love and grief,
Left all alone in the yoke.=

But come, Persians,                              140
Let us in this ancient palace sit,
And deep and wisely found our thoughts:
How does King Xerxes fare, Darius' son,
How fare his people? Has arrows' hail
Or strength of spear conquered?                  150
But lo! she comes,
A light whose splendor equals eyes of gods,
The mother of our king, I kneel.
Now all must address and salute her.

61

(*Enter Queen.*)

O most majestic Queen of Persians
In ample folds adorned,
Hail, agèd Xerxes' mother,
Consort of Darius, hail!
Mistress of the god of Persians,
Mother of a god thou art,
Unless the fortune of their arms
Now at last has altered.

*Queen*

Leaving my gold-clad palace, marriage-
Chamber of Darius, and my own,                                    160
His queen I'm come. Care quite grates my heart;
I fear, my friends, though not fearful for myself,
Lest great wealth's gallop trip prosperity—
Exalted by Darius and some god—
In its own dust. But, unexpectedly,
That dread has doubled: sums of cowardly
Wealth do court contempt, and indigence
Quenches ambition's flame, even if there's strength.
Though wealth we have unstinted; yet fear
Is for mine eye, Xerxes, whose presence here
I count the palace-eye. So things stand thus.           170
Advise my reason, Persians, old sureties:
All my gains with your counsel lie.

*Chorus*

O Queen of Persia, be assured that never
Twice hast thou to tell us word or deed,
Which our willing strength can guide; for we
Are loyal, whom thou dost call thy counselors.

*Queen*

With frequent, constant, and nocturnal dreams
I have lived, as soon as my son, gathering
His host had gone, his will to pillage Greece;

But never a more vivid presence came
Than yesternight's.                                          180
Two women as an apparition came,
One in Persian robes instructed well,
The other Doric, both in splendor dressed,
Who grand and most magnificent excelled
Us now, their beauty unreproached, spotless;
Sisters they, who casting for their father's land,
She Greece received, she Asia, where to dwell.
Then strife arose between them, or so I dreamed;
And my son, observing this, tries to check          190
And soothe them; he yokes them to a chariot,
Bridles their necks: and one, so arrayed, towers
Proud, her mouth obedient to reins;
But the other stamps, annoyed, and rends apart
Her trappings in her hands; unbridled, seizes
The car and snaps its yoke in two;
My son falls, and his father, pitying,
Stands by his side, but at whose sight Xerxes
Tears his robes. Thus in the night these visions
Dreamed: but when, arisen, I touched the springs'          200
Fair-flowing waters, approached the altar, wishing
To offer sacrifice religiously
To guardian deities, whose rites these are,
Then to Phoebus' hearth I saw an eagle fleeing:
Dumb in dread I stood: a falcon swooped
Upon him, its wings in flight, its claws plucked
At his head: he did no more than cower, hare-like.
Those were my terrors to see, and yours to hear.          210
My son, should he succeed, would be admired;
But if he fails, Persia cannot hold him
To account. Whichever comes, safe returned, sovereign
He shall rule.

*Chorus*

       Queen mother, excessive fear
Or confidence we do not wish to give thee.

If thy dreams were ominous, approach
The gods with supplications; pray that these
Be unfulfilled, and blessings be fulfilled
For thee, thy son, thy city, and thy friends.
Next thou must libations pour to Earth
And dead; and beg Darius, of whom thou didst dream,    220
Send thee those blessings from the nether world
To light, for thee and for thy son; and hide
In darkness evils contrary, retained
Within the earth. Propitious be thy prayers.
We, prophetic in our spirit, kindly
Counsel thee: all will prosper.

*Queen*

Ah, loyally have answered the first expounders
Of my dreams. May these blessings ripen!
And all, as you enjoin, I'll sacrifice
To nether gods and friends, as soon as I
Return. But one thing more I wish to know:    230
My friends, where is Athens said to be?

*Chorus*

Far toward the dying flames of sun.

*Queen*

Yet still my son lusts to track it down?

*Chorus*

Then all Hellas would be subject to the king.

*Queen*

So rich in numbers are they?

*Chorus*

                    So great a host
As dealt to Persians many woes.

*Queen*
   Are bow-plucked shafts their armament?

*Chorus*
   Pikes wielded-close and shielded panoplies.

*Queen*
   What else besides? Have they sufficing wealth?          240

*Chorus*
   Their earth is veined with silver treasuries.

*Queen*
   Who commands them? Who is shepherd of their host?

*Chorus*
   They are slaves to none, nor are they subject.

*Queen*
   But how could they withstand a foreign foe?

*Chorus*
   Enough to vanquish Darius' noble host.

*Queen*
   We mothers dread to calculate—

*Chorus*
   But soon thou'lt know all: a Persian runner comes,
   Bearing some fresh report of weal or woe.

(*Enter Herald.*)

*Herald*
   O cities of Asia, O Persian land,
   And wealth's great anchorage!
   How at a single stroke prosperity's          250

Corrupted, and the flower of Persia falls,
And is gone. Alas! the first herald of woe,
He must disclose entire what befell:
Persians, all the barbarian host is gone.

*Chorus*

O woe! woeful evil,
Novel and hostile.
Alas! Persians weep
Hearing this woe.—

*Herald*

How all has been destroyed, and I behold                260
The unexpected light of my return.

*Chorus*

Oh long seems our aged
Life to us elders,
Alas! hearing woe
Unexpected.=

*Herald*

And since I was witness, deaf to rumor's tales,
I can indicate what sorrows came.

*Chorus*

Woe upon woe, in vain
The crowd of arrows, massed,                270
Came on the hostile land.—

*Herald*

The lifeless rotting corpses glut the shore,
And adjacent fields of Salamis.

*Chorus*

Woe upon woe, of friends

66

The sea-dyed corpses whirl
Vagrant on craggèd shores.=

*Herald*
    The bow protected none, but all the host,
    Defeated in the naval charge, was lost.

*Chorus*
    Raise a mournful, doleful cry              280
    For Persians wretched:
    All they made all woe.
    Alas! the host destroyed.—

*Herald*
    O most hateful name of Salamis!
    O woe! how I mourn recalling Athens.

*Chorus*
    Athens hateful to her foes.
    Recall how many
    Persians widowed vain,
    And mothers losing sons.=

*Queen*
    Long am I silent, alas! struck down
    By disasters exceeding speech and question.     290
    Yet men perforce god-sent misfortunes must
    Endure. Speak, disclose entire what
    Befell, quietly, though you grieve.
    Who did not die? For whom of the captains
    Shall we lament? Whose sceptered death drained his
       ranks
    Manless?

*Herald*
            Xerxes lives to behold the light, but—

*Queen*

    O for my palace a greater light,
    And after blackest night a whiter day.          300

*Herald*

    Artembares, captain of ten thousand
    Horse, was dashed against Silenia's
    Rugged shore; and satrap Dadakes,
    Spear-struck, did lightly tumble from his ship;
    And native-born Tenagon, the bravest
    Bactrian, still haunts sea-buffeted
    Ajax' isle; and Lilaeus, Arsames,
    And Argestes, conquered near the island
    Where doves do thrive, beat a stubborn coast;      310
    And neighbors of Egyptian Nile-waters,
    Adeues, Arkteus, and, third, shielded
    Pharnouchus, from a single ship
    Were drowned; and Matallus, satrap of Chrysa,
    Dying, leader of a thousand horse,
    Changed to richest red his thickset flowing
    Beard, and dipped his skin in crimson dyes;
    And Magian Arabus and Bactrian
    Artabes, all aliens in a savage
    Country, perished; Amphistreus, who wielded
    The much-belaboring spear, and Amistris,      320
    Brave Ariomardus, all made Sardis weep;
    And Mysian Seisames, Tharybis,
    Commander of five times fifty ships,
    His race Lyrnaean, fair to look upon
    (His fortune was not), dead he lies;
    And the leader of Cilicians single-handed
    Taxed the enemy with toil, and nobly
    Died. So many of the rulers I
    Recall, but of the many woes, report
    But few.          330

*Queen*

        Alas! I hear the greatest

Of misfortunes, shame of Persians, and shrill
Lament. But tell me, returning to your tale,
What was the number of the Grecian ships,
That thought themselves a match for Persian
Arms in naval combat?

*Herald*

Had numbers counted,
The barbarian warships surely would have won;
The Greeks but numbered thirty tens, and ten          340
Apart from these a chosen squadron formed;
But Xerxes, and this I know full well, a thousand
Led; and seven and two hundred ranked
As queens in swiftness. The count stood so.
Seemed we unequal? Some deity destroyed
Our host, who weighing down the balance swung
The beam of fortune. The gods saved the city
Of the goddess.

*Queen*

What? Athens still
Stands unsacked?

*Herald*

As long as there are men
The city stands.

*Queen*

What was the beginning          350
Of disaster? Tell me. Who began?
The Greeks? My son—exultant in his numbers?

*Herald*

Either an avenger or a wicked
God, my Lady (whence it came I know not),
Began the whole disaster. From Athenian
Ranks a Greek approached, addressing Xerxes

Thus: "When the gloom of blackest night
Will fall, the Greeks will not remain, but leap
To rowing-bench, and each by secret course
Will save his life." And he your son, upon          360
His hearing this, in ignorance of Greek
Guile and the jealousy of gods,
Harangued his captains publicly: "As soon
As sunlit rays no longer burn the earth,
And darkness sweeps the quarters of the sky,
Rank the swarm of ships in three flotillas,
Guard they the entrances, the straits sea-pound,
And girdle others round Ajax' isle;
But if the Greeks escape their evil doom,            370
Contriving secret flight, all your heads
Will roll. I warrant it." So he spoke
In humored pride: of the god-given future
Nothing he knew. And, having supped, they set
Themselves in order, each heart obedient;
And sailors bound a thong about each oar.
When the glare of sunlight died, and night
Came on, every man was at his oar,
Every man at arms who knew them.
Rank encouraged rank, and long-boats sailed          380
To stations each had been assigned.
All night the captains kept the fleet awake;
And night ran on. No Grecian army set
Secret sail: but when the steeds of day,
White and luminous, began to cross
The sky, a song-like, happy tumult sounded
From the Greeks, and island rocks returned          390
The high-pitched echo. Fear fell among us,
Deceived in hope; for they (and not as if to flee)
A solemn paean chanted, and to battle
Rushed with fervent boldness: trumpets flared,
Putting every Greek aflame. At once
Concordant strokes of oars in dissonance
Slapped the waters' depths: soon we saw

Them all: first the right wing led in order,
Next advanced the whole armada;                          400
A great concerted cry we heard: "O Greek
Sons, advance! Free your fathers' land,
Free your sons, your wives, the sanctuaries
Of paternal gods, the sepulchers
Of ancestors. Now the contest's drawn:
All is at stake!" And babel Persian tongues
Rose to meet it: no longer would the action
Loiter. Warships struck their brazen beaks
Together: a Grecian man-of-war began
The charge, a Phoenician ornamented stern        410
Was smashed; another drove against another.
First the floods of Persians held the line,
But when the narrows choked them, and rescue hopeless,
Smitten by prows, their bronze jaws gaping,
Shattered entire was our fleet of oars.
The Grecian warships, calculating, dashed
Round, and encircled us; ships showed their belly:
No longer could we see the water, charged
With ships' wrecks and men's blood.                      420
Corpses glutted beaches and the rocks.
Every warship urged its own anarchic
Rout; and all who survived that expedition,
Like mackerel or some catch of fish,
Were stunned and slaughtered, boned with broken oars
And splintered wrecks: lamentations, cries
Possessed the open sea, until the black
Eye of evening, closing, hushed them. The sum
Of troubles, even if I should rehearse them
For ten days, I could not exhaust. Rest              430
Content: never in a single day
So great a number died.

Queen
    Alas! a sea of troubles breaks in waves
    On the Persians and barbarian tribes.

71

*Herald*

But what we've told would scarcely balance woes
Untold: misfortune came upon them, which
Swung the beam to weigh them double these.

*Queen*

But what greater hatred could fortune show?
What misfortune came upon the soldiers,
Swinging the beam of troubles to greater woes?          440

*Herald*

All the Persians, who were in nature's prime,
Excellent in soul, and nobly bred to grandeur,
Always first in trust, met their death
In infamy, dishonor, and in ugliness.

*Queen*

Oh, wretched am I, alas! What doom
Destroyed them?

*Herald*

There is an island fronting Salamis,
Small, scarce an anchorage for ships,
Where the dancer Pan rejoices on the shore;
Whither Xerxes sent those men to kill                   450
The shipwrecked enemies who sought the island
As a refuge (easily, he thought,
The Grecian arms would be subdued);
He also bid them rescue friends. He conned
The future ill. For when a god gave Greeks
The glory, that very day, fenced in bronze,
They leaped ashore, and drew the circle tight
At every point: mewed up, we could not turn.
Many rattled to the ground, whom stones
Had felled, and arrows, shot by bowstring,              460
Others killed; and in a final rush,
The end: they hacked, mangled their wretched limbs,

Until the life of all was gone.
Xerxes mourned, beholding the lowest depths
Of woe; who, seated on a height that near
The sea commanded all his host, his robes
Destroying (and his lamentations shrill),
Dispatched his regiments on land: they fled          470
Orderless. Now you may lament their fate,
Added to the others' summed before.

Queen

O hateful deity! how the Persians
You deceived! Bitter was the vengeance
Which my son at famous Athens found:
She could not sate her appetite with those
Whom Marathon had made the Persians lose.
For these my son, exacting as requital
Punishment (or so he thought)
Called on himself so numerous
A train of woes. Tell me, what ships escaped?
Where are they now? Can you clearly tell?

Herald

Who captained the remaining ships set sail          480
Before the wind, fleeing in disorder;
But the army perished in Boeotia: some,
In want of precious water, were racked with thirst,
And some, gasping emptily on air,
Crossed to Phocis, Locria, the Malian
Gulf, where Spercheian waters kindly drench
The plain; and thence Achaea and Thessaly
Received us, wanting: there most died          490
In hunger and in thirst: both we felt.
To Magnesia and Macedonia we came,
The River Axius, the reedy marsh
Of Bolba, the mountain Pangaeon,
And Thrace. There in the night a god
Roused winter out of season: all, who had

73

Believed the gods were naught, sang their chants,
To earth and sky obeisance made.
When we ceased invoking gods, we tried                    500
Waters that had turned to ice:
Whoever started before Apollo's rays
Spread and scattered in the sky, he
Was saved. Soon the brilliant orb of sun,
Its ray aflame, melts the river's midst:
One falls upon the next: happy he whose life
Was first cut short! The rest did make their way         510
But painfully through Thrace: not many fled
To hearth and home. Thus the city of Persians
May lament, regretting the loss of youth.
Truthful I have been, but omit many
Of the woes a god has hurled against
The Persians.

(*Exit Herald.*)

*Chorus*

       O toilsome deity! how heavily
You leaped upon all Persia!

*Queen*

Alas! woe is me, the host destroyed.
O bright night's spectacle of dreams,
How clearly you foresaw my woe,
And you, my counselors, how poorly judged.                520
But yet, as you counseled thus,
First to the gods I'll offer prayer; and then
To Earth and dead I'll come to offer gifts,
A sacrificial cake. I know I pray
For what is done and gone, but a brighter
Fortune, in time to come, may there be.
And you, worthy of trust, exchange worthy counsel;
My son, should he return before my own

74

Return, comfort and escort him home:
I fear to woes he'll add more woe.                              530

                                        (*Exit Queen.*)

*Chorus*
   O! royal Zeus destroyed
   The multitudinous, proud
   Host of the Persian men,
   And the cities of Sousa
   And of Agbatana
   Concealed in the darkness of grief.

   Many with delicate hands
   Rending their veils,
   Drenching their breasts,
   Swollen with tears,                                540
   Sharing their woe,
   Ladies of Persia
   Softly are weeping,
   Desiring each
   Him to behold
   Wedded but lately,
   Couches forsaking,
   Soft as their coverlets
   (Youth was voluptuous),
   Their sorrows, insatiate woe.
   And I the paean's song recite,
   Doom of the gone,
   Woe upon woe.

   Now all Asia
   Desolate, void,
   Sighs lament:
   Xerxes led,                                      550
   Alas,
   Xerxes lost,

O woe,
Xerxes heedless all discharged
With ocean argosies.
Why was Darius so long without harm,
Archery's captain of citizens,
Loved Sousa's lord? —

Armies, navies
Lazuli-eyed,
Linen-winged                                                    560
Warships led,
O woe,
Warships rammed destructively
By Grecian arms.
Scarcely escaped was the leader alone
(So we have heard) in the Thracian
Plains, bitter ways. =

They of the first death,
Alas,
Left by necessity,
Woe,
Round by Kychraean shores,                                      570
Oh,
Moan in your anguish,
Cry to the heavens your grief,
Oh,
Wail long-weeping
Mournful cries. —

Torn in the sea-swirl,
Alas,
Mangled by voiceless,
Woe,
Fish of the unstained sea.
Oh,
Houses deprived grieve,

76

Sonless, to heavens their grief,                                        580
Oh,
Elders mourning,
Hear all woe.=

They throughout the Asian land
No longer Persian laws obey,
No longer lordly tribute yield,
Exacted by necessity;
Nor suffer rule as suppliants,
To earth obeisance never make:
Lost is the kingly power.—                                            590

Nay, no longer is the tongue
Imprisoned kept, but loose are men,
When loose the yoke of power's bound,
To bawl their liberty.
But Ajax' isle, spilled with blood
Its earth, and washed round by sea,
Holds the remains of Persia.=

                                        (*Enter Queen.*)

*Queen*
  My friends, whoever's wise in ways of evil
  Knows how, when a flood of evil comes,
  Everything we grow to fear; but when                                600
  A god our voyage gladdens, we believe
  Always that fortune's never-changing wind
  Will blow. As my eyes behold all things
  As fearful visitations of the gods,
  So my ears already ring with cureless songs:
  Thus consternation terrifies my sense.
  Therefore I departed from the palaces,
  Alone returning, unaccompanied
  By chariots, by pomp and ceremony.
  To the father of my son I bring

Propitious offerings, libations                                        610
For the dead: a milk-sweet draught of sacred kine
Unblemished; and resplendent liquors of the honey-
Working bee, with liquid droplets of a maiden
Stream are mingled; and this elixir
Of an antique vine, whose mother is
The wild fields; and golden-green the fruit
Of fragrant olive trees, always flourishing
Their leafy age; and plaited flowers, children
Of the fecund earth. My friends, recite
Your chants and threnodies; recall
Darius' demon over these libations                                     620
To the dead, sepulchral honors, which
I lavish on the nether gods.

*Chorus*

O Queen of the Persians,
To the dark chambers
Libations pour;
While, kindness imploring
Of the gods, the conductors,
We offer prayer:
Ye sacred divinities,
Earth and King Hermes,                                                 630
Conduct him to light
Up from the dead,
Who alone of all mortals,
A remedy knowing,
May show us the end.

Hearest thou, blessèd king
Equal to god,
As I proclaim now
Chantings unpleasant
Barbarous mournful
Clear and diverse?
Miserable sorrows

I shall cry out.
Below dost thou hearken?—

Earth and the other gods                               640
Leaders of dead,
Glorious demon
Him let arise thence,
God of the Persians
Sousa his mother;
Send up the man whom
Never surpassed
The Persian land buried.=

Loved is the man, loved his tomb
Hiding his loving ways.
Aedoneus conductor,
Would that Aedoneus send                               650
Lord Darius alone:—

Never by war wasted his men,
Never infatuate,
Called a god in wisdom,
God in wisdom he was,
Ruled his people well.=

Padshah, ancient Padshah,
Appear on the height of thy tomb,
Raise thy slipper saffron-dyed,                        660
Flash the lappets of thy crown:
Father Darius, Oh hither come, woe.—

Hear the recent sorrows,
O master of masters appear.
Stygian gloom doth flit about;
All the youth hath perished now.                       670
Father Darius, Oh hither come, woe.=

79

Oh, alas, Oh!
O much-lamented by his friends in death:
The ships with triple banks of oars are gone.　　　　680

*(The Ghost of Darius rises.)*

*Darius*

O faithful followers, companions
Of my youth! O Persian counselors!
What burden's burdening the city, which
In lamentation moans, and makes the plains
Tremble? And terrified I saw my wife
Beside my tomb, and graciously received
Her offerings; and you lamented, standing
Near my tomb, with cries of resurrection
Calling piteously. Ascent is not easy.
The chthonic deities more readily　　　　　　　690
Receive than give; but I, a potentate
Among them, came: be quick, that I be un-
Reproached for being late. What recent woe
Upon the Persians weighs?

*Chorus*

I'm shamed to behold thee,
I'm shamed to address thee,
Who was anciently feared.—

*Darius*

Since I have risen obeying
Lamentations, lengthen not
Your tale, but speak succinctly,
Recounting all. Lay aside your
Reverence toward me.

*Chorus*

I tremble to please thee,

I tremble to tell thee
What is loth to be told.= 700

Darius

As an ancient fear obstructs your sense,
You, agèd consort of my marriage,
Noble Queen, cease your weeping; tell me
Clearly: many woes arise by sea, many
Come by land, the longer life is racked.

Queen

O King, exceeding mortal happiness
By happy fate! How, as long as you beheld
The eyes of sun, you spent, how envied! a blessed 710
Life like god's; and now I envy you
Your dying, ere you saw this depth of woe.
Everything, Darius, you will hear
Succinctly: Persia is destroyed.

Darius

How? A lightning-bolt of hunger? Civil
Strife within the city?

Queen

No, but all
The host's destroyed at Athens.

Darius

Who among
My sons was general? Tell me.

Queen

Furious Xerxes, who drained the plain manless.

Darius

By foot or warship was his vain attempt?

**Queen**
By both: a double front of doubled hosts.

**Darius**
But how did so great an army cross the strait?

**Queen**
Devices, yoking Helle's strait, a path
Afforded.

**Darius**
          He accomplished this? To close
Great Bosphorus?

**Queen**
                    So it was; some god
Contrived it..

**Darius**
              Alas! a great divinity
Deceived his sense.

**Queen**
                    The evil end he made
Is present to the eye.

**Darius**
                    What befell them
That you thus lament?

**Queen**
                      The naval host,
Destroyed, destroyed the landed host.

**Darius**
Thus all the people spears destroyed.

**Queen**
Thus Sousa groans desolate.                                     730

**Darius**
Alas! the goodly host! Alas! defenders!

**Queen**
All the Bactrians destroyed, no youth remains.

**Darius**
O woe! the youth of allies gone.

**Queen**
                              Xerxes
Alone with few they say.

**Darius**
                         Perished how?
Perished where?

**Queen**
                    To the joyous bridge
They came, the yoke of continents.

**Darius**
He was saved? Can this be true?

**Queen**
Yes, a clear report without dispute.

**Darius**
Alas! that prophecy was quick to act!
Zeus hurled against my son its lightning-end,          740
While I expected after many years
The gods would make an end; but when a man's
Willing and eager, god joins in. The spring
Of evil's found: my son in ignorance

Discovered it, by youthful pride; who hoped
To check the sacred waters of the Hellespont
By chains, just as if it were a slave. He smoothed
His way, yoking Neptune's flowing Bosphorus
With hammered shackles. Mortal though he was,
By folly thought to conquer all the gods
And Neptune. Had not my son diseased his sense?          750
I fear my labored wealth will fall the prey
Of conquerors.

Queen

        Wicked men counseled this, furious
Xerxes learned; saying you acquired wealth
By spear, while he, in cowardice, played
The warrior at home, and multiplied
By nothing his ancestral wealth. So often
These wicked men reproached him, until he
Did plot his martial way toward Greece.

Darius

So their great, eternal deed is done!
Never had anyone before made this          760
Sousa so empty and so desolate,
Since Zeus, our Lord, bestowed that honor:
One man to wield his rod's authority
Over all of Asia, rich in flocks.
First was Medus leader of the host;
Next his son fulfilled the office well,
Whose reason was the helmsman to his spirit;
Third was Cyrus, fortunate, whose rule
Brought peace to all: the Lydian people
And the Phrygian he acquired,          770
And marched his might against Ionia:
No god resented him, for he was wise;
And fourth was Cyrus' son, who shamed his country
And ancestral throne; but Artaphrenes
(Aided by his guile) and his friends,

Whose task this was, slew him in his palace.
After him, I, willing, drew the lot
To rule, and often led a mighty host;                    780
But never did I cast so great a woe
Upon my city. Xerxes, my son, as young
In age as sense, ignored my wisdom. Know
This well, my comrades old as I, all of us
Who held these powers, never wrought so many
Woes.

*Chorus*
       To what end, my Lord Darius, dost thou
Harp on this? How could we, the Persian
People, fare the best?

*Darius*
               If you lead
No expedition to the land of Greece,                     790
Not even if the Median host be more;
For Grecian soil is their own ally.

*Chorus*
What dost thou intend by that, "their own ally"?

*Darius*
It starves to death excessive numbers.

*Chorus*
But, be sure, we'll raise a well-equipped
And chosen host.

*Darius*
               But even they, who now
Remain in Greece, shall find no safe return.

*Chorus*
What? Shall not all the host return
Across the strait of Helle?

*Darius*
                              Few of many,
If the oracles of gods are credited:                          800
As we gaze at what has passed, no half
Prophecy succeeds, but either all
Or none. If we credit them, he leaves
Behind, his empty hopes persuading, chosen
Numbers of his host, who now are stationed
Where Asopus floods the plain, its rich sap
Kind to Boeotia; here await them
The lowest depths of woe to suffer, payment
For his pride and godless arrogance.
They, invading Greece, felt no awe,
They did not hesitate to plunder images
Of gods, and put temples to the torch;                        810
Altars were no more, and statues, like trees,
Were uprooted, torn from their bases
In all confusion. Thus their wickedness
Shall no less make them suffer:
Other woes the future holds in store,
And still the fount of evils is not quenched,
It wells up, and overflows: so great will be
The sacrificial cake of clotted gore
Made at Plataea by Dorian spear.
And corpses, piled up like sand, shall witness,
Mute, even to the century to come,
Before the eyes of men, that never, being
Mortal, ought we cast our thoughts too high.                  820
Insolence, once blossoming, bears
Its fruit, a tasseled field of doom, from which
A weeping harvest's reaped, all tears.
Behold the punishment of these! remember
Greece and Athens! lest you disdain
Your present fortune, and lust after more,
Squandering great prosperity.
Zeus is the chastener of overboastful
Minds, a grievous corrector. Therefore advise

Him, admonished by reason, to be wise, 830
And cease his overboastful temper from
Sinning against the gods. And you, aged
Mother of Xerxes, go to the palace;
Gather up rich and brilliant cloths, and go
To meet your son; for he, in grief, has rent
His embroidered robes to shreds. Gently soothe
Him with your words: to yours alone he'll listen.
Now shall I descend to nether gloom.
Elder counselors, farewell, and though
In time of troubles, give daily pleasures 840
To your soul, as wealth cannot benefit
The dead.

*(The Ghost of Darius descends.)*

*Chorus*

Alas! the woes upon us and the woes
To come have grieved me hearing them.

*Queen*

O god! how many sorrows move against me!
But one torment has the deepest fang,
Hearing that dishonor folds about my son
Its robes. But I shall go to gather up
Adornments, and try to meet my son. 850
When evils come on those we dearly love,
Never shall we betray them.

*(Exit Queen.)*

*Chorus*

Oh! alas, Oh! what a great and a good life was ours,
Civilly ordered, as long as the agèd
Ruler of all,
Mild, unconquerable king,

87

Equal to god,
Darius ruled the land.—

Glorious arms we displayed, and the bulwarks of custom
All they did guide. And returning from battle                860
Grief had we none,
Victors, unburdened of all,
Happy and glad,
To home again we came.=

For many the cities he sacked never crossing the Halys,
Nor leaving his hearth in a rush:
At the mouth of the River Strymon,
Near Thracian places,
The islands of Achelous;—

Both cities beyond the Aegean, surrounded by towers,    870
Obeyed him our lord, and who round
The broad strait of Helle boasting,
And recessed Propontis,
And gateway of Pontus, Bosphor;=

And the isles along the headland washed by sea          880
Lying close to shore:
Samos and Chios and Lesbos the olive-planted,
Paros and Naxos and Mykonos,
And Tenos the neighbor of Andros.—

And the islands in the midst of sea he ruled:
Ikaros and Lemnos,                                      890
Rhodus and Knidos and cities of Aphrodite,
Paphos and Solus and Salamis,
Whose founder's the cause of these sorrows.=

Thus the wealthy and populous lands,
The Ionian province, he ruled;                          900
And the strength of his helmeted men

Was unwearied, innumerable allies.
But now we bear god-routed fortunes,
Overcome by the blows of the sea.

(*Enter Xerxes alone.*)

*Xerxes*

Oh, hateful this doom, woe is me,
Wretched alas, without augury.                          910
How savagely swooped the deity.
What will befall me? I swoon
Beholding these citizens agèd.
Zeus! would that fate had covered me
With the Persians gone!

*Chorus*

Oh alas, King, for a brave host,
For the great honor of Persian rule,
For the ranks of men whom a god has slain.             920

Nations wail their native sons,
Who by Xerxes stuffed up hell;
Many heroes, Persia's bloom,
Archers, thick array of men,
Myriads have perished.
Woe, O King of noble strength.
Cruel! Cruel! Asia kneels.                              930

*Xerxes*

Here am I, alas, O woe:
To my native and ancestral land
Woe is the evil I've become.

*Chorus*

Loudly shall I send, for your return,
An evil-omened shout, an evil-practiced cry:
A weeping wail of Persian mourners shall I sing.—

*Xerxes*

Send a wail of evil sound
Lamenting and grievous: now
Fortune again has changed for me.                              940

*Chorus*

Mourning wail all-weeping shall I send,
In honor of your woes and sea-struck grief:
Again a wailing filled with tears I'll cry.=

*Xerxes*

Ionian Ares spoiled,
Protected by their ships,                                      950
Their partisan in war,
Reaping gloomy flats of sea
    and demon-haunted shores.

*Chorus*

Oh alas!

*Xerxes*

            Lament and ask for all.

*Chorus*

But where are the others?
Where is thy retinue,
Like Pharandakas,
Sousas, Pelagon, and Agabatas,
Dotamas, Psammis, Sousiscanes                                 960
Leaving Agbatana?—

*Xerxes*

The lost I deserted there,
Who from the ships of Tyre
To Salaminian shore
Vanished and were gone, their corpses
    pounding stubborn shores.

*Chorus*

    Oh alas! but where is Pharnouchus
    And brave Ariomardus?
    Where is Seualkes lord,
    Or Lilaeus grand,
    Memphis, Tharybis, and Masistres,         970
    Artembares and Hystaechmes?
    These I ask you about.=

*Xerxes*

    Oh alas, woe,
    Who all, beholding ancient, hateful Athens, gasp on
        shore,
    Woe upon woe, wretched in a single sweep of oar.

*Chorus*

    Did you leave that Persian there,
    Your trusted universal eye,         980
    Who made his count by myriads,
    Batanochus' son Alpistus?

    .  .  .  .  .  .  .

    Of Sesames, of Megabates,
    Great Parthus and Oebares you left behind?
    O woe, O woe, O miseries.
    You tell of woes on woes.—

*Xerxes*

    Oh alas, woe,         990
    The magic wheel of longing for my friends you turn, you
        tell
    Me hateful sorrows. Within my frame my heart resounds,
        resounds.

*Chorus*

    And for the others still we long:
    The leader of ten thousand men
    Of Mardia, Xanthes, Angchares,

And Diaexis and Arsamas,
Masters of horsemen,
And Dadakas and Lythimnas,
And Tolmus who never slaked his spear.
I see about the moving tents,                          1000
I see no followers.=

*Xerxes*
Gone are the hunters of the pack.

*Chorus*
Gone, alas, fameless.

*Xerxes*
Oh alas, woe.

*Chorus*
Woe, O gods
Who brought these unexpected woes!
How baleful gleams the eye of doom.—

*Xerxes*
Struck by woes perpetual.

*Chorus*
Struck by recent—

*Xerxes*
A recent woe.                                          1010

*Chorus*
Woe, alas,
They met the men-of-war without success:
How luckless was the Persians' war.=

*Xerxes*
Alas, in so vast an army I am struck.

92

*Chorus*
  What is not lost, thou curse of the Persians?

*Xerxes*
  Behold the remnants of my power

*Chorus*
  I see, I see.

*Xerxes*
  And this receptacle.                                    1020

*Chorus*
  What is this that is saved?

*Xerxes*
  A treasure of arrows.

*Chorus*
  How few from so many!

*Xerxes*
  We are reft of protectors.

*Chorus*
  Greeks stand firm in combat.—

*Xerxes*
  Alas, too firm! I scan an unexpected woe.

*Chorus*
  You mean the host, routed and broken?

*Xerxes*
  My garments I rent at my woe.

*Chorus*
  Alas, O woe.                                            1030

*Xerxes*
And even more than woe.

*Chorus*
Double and triple the woe.

*Xerxes*
Painful to us, but to enemies joy.

*Chorus*
And docked was our power.

*Xerxes*
I am stripped of escorters.

*Chorus*
Sea-dooms stripped us of our friends. =

*Xerxes*
Weep, weep, weep for the woe, and homeward depart.

*Chorus*
Alas, O woe, misery.

*Xerxes*
Shout antiphonal to me.                                    1040

*Chorus*
To woebegone woeful gift of woes.

*Xerxes*
Raising a cry, join together our songs.

*Xerxes and Chorus*
Alas, O woe, woe, woe upon woe.

*Chorus*
Hearing this calamity,
Oh! I am pierced.—

*Xerxes*
Sweep, sweep, sweep with the oar, and groan for my sake.

*Chorus*
I weep, alas, woe is me.

*Xerxes*
Shout antiphonal to me.

*Chorus*
My duty is here, O master, lord.

*Xerxes*
Lift up your voice in lamenting now.                    1050

*Xerxes and Chorus*
Alas, O woe, woe, woe upon woe.

*Chorus*
Black again the blows are mixed,
Oh, with the groans.=

*Xerxes*
Beat your breast and cry Mysian songs.

*Chorus*
Woe upon woe.

*Xerxes*
Tear your whitened hair tightly clenched.

*Chorus*
  Tightly clenched, plaintive.

*Xerxes*
  Piercing cry.

*Chorus*
  And so I shall.—

*Xerxes*
  Full-fold garments with strength of hand rend.          1060

*Chorus*
  Woe upon woe.

*Xerxes*
  Pluck your hair and pity the host.

*Chorus*
  Tightly clenched, plaintive.

*Xerxes*
  Drench your eyes.

*Chorus*
  And so I weep.=

*Xerxes*
  Shout antiphonal to me.

*Chorus*
  Alas, O woe.

*Xerxes*
  Wretched, homeward depart.

*Chorus*
  O woe, alas.                                      1070

*Xerxes*
  Through the city lamentation.

*Chorus*
  Lament indeed.

*Xerxes*
  Softly stepping, moan.

*Chorus*
  O Persian land in hardness stepped.

*Xerxes*
  O woe, woe, in triple banks of oars,
  O woe, woe, in argosies destroyed.

*Chorus*
  We shall escort thee
  With mournful lament.

                                      *(Exit all.)*

# SEVEN AGAINST THEBES

*Translated and with an Introduction by*

DAVID GRENE

# INTRODUCTION TO
## SEVEN AGAINST THEBES

This strange, archaic play was produced in 467 B.C. It is probably the last play of a trilogy written by Aeschylus on the theme of the Oedipus cycle. It is at once undramatic and yet, in a paradoxical way, very theatrical. Who can take seriously a play with almost no action, in which the main event is the recital of the blazonry on the shields of the Seven Champions? But a careful reading will reveal the tremendous effect that the dancing accompaniments would have made. The effect of the whole is, despite its disadvantages for a modern reader, very powerful.

The play is extremely hard to translate. The style is heroic in the good parts and bombastic in the bad. It is never simple and luminous. Whereas the same quality of diction in the elevated parts of the *Prometheus* is always suited to a majesty of theme comprehensible to a modern reader, the matter of the *Seven* is remote from the interest of a reader today, and it needs imagination to conceive of it in the Greek theater, let alone on the stage as we now know it.

It is perhaps better understood by a modern reader in the mood in which he would now attend a ritual ceremony, a church service, or a pageant such as the coronation of an English monarch. The recital of the devices on the shields, the matching of the champions, and, in the last part of the play, the antiphonal keening of the sisters over the dead bodies of their brothers are all properly traditional ritual. They were probably filled for the Greek spectator with matter pertinent to his own time. The political relation of Argos,

Thebes, and Athens was then much discussed, and Aeschylus has undoubtedly used the popular interest in these matters to render the old story vital for his audience. It may be that the names of the champions had many associations for the mid-fifth-century Greek. Aeschylus has similarly used the general interest in the Areopagus in the years 462-459 B.C. for the pageant drama of the *Oresteia*. Though many of the clues to his employment of this method in the *Seven* are lost to us, we are almost certainly correct in assuming that this is again the course he adopted. The *Seven*, like the *Eumenides*, is the last play of the trilogy, and in both Aeschylus has managed to raise progressively a particular story to the level of a general process of history culminating in a particular historical occurrence known to his contemporaries.

## CHARACTERS

*Eteocles, son of Oedipus and*
  *present ruler of Thebes*
*Antigone*⎫
         ⎬ *his sisters*
*Ismene*  ⎭
*Messenger*
*Chorus of Theban Women*

# SEVEN AGAINST THEBES

SCENE: *Thebes. The Prince Eteocles confronts a crowd of Thebans.*

*Eteocles*
　You citizens of Cadmus, he must speak home
　that in the ship's prow watches the event
　and guides the rudder, his eye not drooped in sleep.
　For if we win success, the God is the cause
　but if—may it not chance so—there is disaster,
　throughout the town, voiced by its citizens,
　a multitudinous swelling prelude
　cries on one name "Eteocles" with groans:
　which Zeus defender keep from the city of Cadmus
　even as his name implies.
　You must help her now—you still something short  **10**
　of your young manhood and you whose time of youth
　is gone, your body grown to its full bigness—
　each of you to such charge as fits you:
　help the city, help the altars of your country's Gods;
　save their honors from destruction:
　help your children, help Earth your Mother.
　She reared you, on her kindly surface, crawling
　babies, welcomed all the trouble of your nurture,
　reared you to live in her, to carry a shield
　in her defense, loyally, against such needs as this.  **20**
　Now to this God kindly inclines this day.
　For those who have been held in siege so long
　the Gods grant commonly a favorable fight.

So says the prophet now, bird shepherding
with skill unlying, ears and mind and fire
tending the oracular birds.
The master of these prophecies declares
enemy's night council framed a plot
for the greatest Achaean assault upon us.
All to the battlements, to the gates of the towers!           30
Haste, in full armor, man the breastworks:
stand on the scaffolding and at the exit gates
be firm, abide, your hearts confident:
fear not that mighty mob of foreigners.
God will dispose all well:
I have sent scouts and spies upon their host:
they will not—well I know it—make the journey
vainly, and by their information
I shall be armed against enemy's stratagems.

*Messenger*

Eteocles, great prince of the Cadmaeans,
I come bringing a clear word from the army           40
of matters there: I myself too
have seen the things I speak of.
There were seven men, fierce regiment commanders,
who cut bulls' throats into an iron-rimmed
shield, and with hands touched the bulls' blood,
taking their oaths by Ares and Enyo,
by the bloodthirsty God of Battle Rout
either to lay your city level
with the ground, sacked, or by their death to make
a bloody paste of this same soil of yours.
Remembrances of themselves for parents at home
their hands have hung upon Adrastus' chariot:           50
their tears ran down,
but never a word of pity was in their mouths.
Their spirits were hard as iron and ablaze
breathed courage: war looked through their lion-eyes.
You will not wait long for confirmation

of this my news: I left them casting lots
how each should lead his regiment against your gates.
Wherefore the choicest men within your city
set at the entrance gates: set them quickly
for near already the armed host of Argives
comes in a cloud of dust, flecks of white,                60
panted from horses' lungs, staining the ground.
You, like the skilful captain of a ship
barricade your town before the blast of Ares
strikes it in storm: already bellows
the armed land wave. Take quickest opportunity
for all these things and I for the rest
will keep my eye, a trusty day watcher.
Thanks to my clear reports you shall know whatever
happens within the gates, and come to no harm.

*Eteocles*

O Zeus and Earth and Gods that guard the city
My father's Curse, mighty evil spirit,                    70
do not root out this city of mine, do not
give her to ruin and destruction, do not
give her to capture nor her homes and hearths.
This is a town that speaks with a Greek tongue.
City and land of the Cadmaeans are free:
do not bind her in slavish yoke; be her protector.
I think I speak for everybody's good,
for a city prosperous honors the Gods.

*Chorus*

My sorrows are great and fearful: I cry aloud:
the army has left the camp and is gone.
Look at the forward rushing river, the great tide of horsemen! 80
I see a cloud of dust, sky high, and am convinced;
a messenger clear and unlying, though voiceless.

Treading feet on the earth of my country,
trampling hoofs, the sound of these draws near.

*(Shout is heard.)*

It floats, it rings
like a resistless mountain waterfall.
O Gods, O Goddesses, the trouble raised!
Turn it aside!

*(Shouts.)*

Over the walls they spring
the Horse of the White Shield
well equipped, hastening upon our city.                    90

Who will protect us? Who will be our champion
of gods or goddesses?
Shall I kneel at the images of the Gods?
O Blessed Ones, throned in peace,
it is time to cling to your images.
We delay and wail too much.

Do you hear or do you not the rattle of shields?          100

When, if not now, shall we hang
robes and garlands on your statues, supplicating?

I see the sound!
No one spear rattled so.

What will you do? Will you betray,
ancient lord of our land Ares,
your own land?

O spirit of the golden helmet look down upon us,
look down upon a city
which once you dearly loved.

City guarding gods of our land, come, come all of you!
Look upon us a band of virgins,                           110
suppliants against slavery!

Around our city the wave of warriors, with waving plumes,
roars; blasts of the War God stirred them.
Alas alas Zeus, Father Omnipotent! all fulfilling!
Let us not fall into the hands of the foeman!
For the Argives are around Cadmus' city.                    120
Fear is stronger than arms.
There is murder in the ringing bits
between their horses' jaws.
Seven proud captains of the host,
with harness and spear,
having won their place by lot,
stand champions at seven gates.
O victory, battle-loving, Zeus begotten,
save our city!

O Pallas, and the Horseman, Prince of the Sea,           130
King of the Trident, Poseidon,
deliverance from fear,
deliverance grant.
You, Ares, protect the city of Cadmus, that bears your
    name.

Show your care for it, in manifest presence.
And Cypris, who are our ancestress                        140
turn destruction away. We are sprung from your blood
we approach you and cry
with prayers for the ears of the Gods.

And you, Wolf God, be a very Wolf
in the enemy host. And you, daughter of Leto,
make ready your bow.

Ah, ah,                                                   150
the rattle of chariots round the city: I hear it.
O Lady Hera,
the groaning axles of the loaded wheels.
Beloved Artemis!

The air is mad with the whirr of spears.
What will happen our city, what will become of it,
whereto shall the Gods bring an end upon us?

There comes a shower of stones on the top of the battle-
    ments!
O beloved Apollo!
There is the rattle of bronze-bound shields at our gates!   160
O Son of Zeus
from whom comes the war's fulfilment,
from whom comes the fight's holy consummation.

O Athene, Blessed Queen, Champion of the city,
deliver her from the assault of the Seven.
O Gods all sufficient,
O Gods and Goddesses, Perfecters,
Protectors of our country's forts,
do not betray this city, spear-won,
to a foreign-tongued enemy.   170
Hear O hear the prayers, hand outstretched,
of the virgins supplicating in justice.

O beloved Spirits,
that encompass our city to its deliverance,
show how much you love it:
Bethink you of the public sacrifices.
As we have thought of you, rescue us.
Remember, I pray you, the rites
with loving sacrifice offered.   180

*Eteocles*

  You insupportable creatures, I ask you,
is this the best, is this for the city's safety,
is this enheartening for our beleaguered army,
to have you falling at the images
of the city's Gods crying and howling,
an object of hatred for all temperate souls?

Neither in evils nor in fair good luck
may I share a dwelling with the tribe of women!
When she's triumphant, hers a confidence
past converse with another, when afraid
an evil greater both for home and city.                           190
Here now running wild among the citizenry
you have roared them into spiritless cowardice.
So, outside of our gates, gains strength the enemy
while we are by ourselves, within, undone.
All this you may have, for living with women.
Now if there is anyone that will not hear
my orders, be he man or woman or in between,
sentence of death shall be decreed against him
and public stoning he shall not escape.
What is outside is a man's province: let no                      200
woman debate it: within doors do no mischief!
Do you hear me or not? Or are you deaf?

*Chorus*

Dear son of Oedipus, the bumping rattle of the chariots,
rattle, rattle, I am afraid when I hear,
when the naves of the axles screech in their running
when the fire-forged bits speak ringingly,
rudder oars in horses' mouths.

*Eteocles*

What, shall the sailor, then, leave the stern
and run to the prow and find device for safety
when his vessel is foundering in the sea waves?            210

*Chorus*

But it was to the images of the Gods
the ancient images I ran, trusting in the Gods,
when the stony snowflakes crashed upon our gates:
nay, then I was lifted up with force and betook me to
    prayer

111

to the Blessed Ones, for our city,
that they may make their strength its protection.

*Eteocles*

For protection pray that our towers
hold off the enemy's spears.

*Chorus*

And shall not that be
as the Gods dispose?

*Eteocles*

            The Gods, they say,
of a captured town desert her.

*Chorus*

Never in my lifetime, never may this assembly
of Gods desert us: never may I live to see          220
this city overrun, an enemy soldiery
putting the torch to it.

*Eteocles*

Do not call upon the Gods
and then be guided wrongly.
Obedience is mother to success,
and success is parent of rescue—
so runs the proverb.

*Chorus*

This is true: but the strength of God is still greater.
Oftentimes when a man is hopelessly sunk
in misfortune He raises him, yes from his greatest sorrow
while the clouds still hang over him, high above our eyes.

*Eteocles*

But it is man's part, the sacrifice, the consultation          230

of the Gods, when the enemy assault us;
it is yours to be silent and stay within doors.

*Chorus*

It is thanks to the Gods that we have our city
unconquered: it is thanks to them
that our towers reject the mob of foemen.
What should be resented in these words?

*Eteocles*

I do not grudge your honoring the Gods.
But lest you make our citizens cowards,
be quiet and not overfearful.

*Chorus*

It was but now that I heard the noise and the confusion
and trembling in fear came to this citadel,                    240
sacred seat.

*Eteocles*

If you shall learn of men dying or wounded,
do not be eager to anticipate it with cries,
for murdered men are the War God's nourishment.

*Chorus*

The snorting of horses! There, I hear it.

*Eteocles*

Do not listen; do not hear too much.

*Chorus*

Our city groans from its foundation: we are surrounded.

*Eteocles*

I shall think of this: that is enough for you.

**Chorus**
I am afraid: the din at the gates grows louder.

**Eteocles**
Silence! Do not speak of this throughout the city.     250

**Chorus**
O Blessed Band, do not betray this fort.

**Eteocles**
Damnation! Can you not endure in silence?

**Chorus**
Fellow-citizen Gods, grant me not to be a slave.

**Eteocles**
It is you who enslave yourselves, and all the city.

**Chorus**
O Zeus, All Mighty, your bolt upon our foes!

**Eteocles**
O Zeus, what a tribe you have given us in women!

**Chorus**
Base is the tribe of men of a captured town.

**Eteocles**
Words of ill omen, your hands on the images!

**Chorus**
Fear captures my tongue, and my spirit is nought.

**Eteocles**
Grant me, I pray you, the small thing I ask.     260

*Chorus*
Speak it quickly, that I may know.

*Eteocles*
Silence, you wretches, don't frighten your friends.

*Chorus*
I am silent: with others I'll endure what is fated.

*Eteocles*
I like this word better than those before.
Furthermore, get you away from the statues,
and being so, utter a better prayer:
"May the Gods stand our allies." First hear my
prayer and then offer yours—
a holy gracious paean of thanksgiving,
the cry of sacrifice, our Grecian custom,
joy to our friends, dissolving fear of foes.                    270

(*He approaches the images himself and prays.*)
Gods of the city, of this country Gods,
Lords of its fields, and its assembly places,
Springs of Dirce, waters of Ismenus—
to you my vow:
if all go well with us, if the city is saved,
my people shall dye your hearths with the blood
of sacrificed sheep, aye with the blood
of bulls slaughtered to honor the Gods.
I shall myself dedicate trophies,
spoils of my enemies, their garments fixed
on spear points, in your sanctuaries.

(*To the Chorus*)
These be your prayers, unlamenting                    280
with no vain wild panting and moaning.
For all such you will not escape your doom.
I will take six men, myself to make a seventh

115

and go to post them at the city's gates,
opponents of the enemy, in gallant style,
before quick messengers are on us and
their words of haste burn us with urgency.

*Chorus*

I heed him but through fear
my spirit knows no sleep:
and neighbors to my heart, 290
anxieties, kindle terror
of the host that beleaguers us.
As the all-fearing dove
dreads for its nestlings' sake
the snakes that menace them.
For they against our forts
with all their host, with all their people,
come. What will become of me?
Jagged rocks they hurl
upon our citizens, on both sides pelted. 300
O children of Zeus, ye Gods,
I pray you—protect
the city and the army,
the Cadmus born.
What country will you take in exchange,
than this one better,
if you abandon this deep-soiled land
to her enemies,
and Dirce's water, fairest to drink
of all that come from Poseidon 310
the Earth Upholder, and Tethys' sons?
Therefore, you city-guarding Gods,
upon the men outside our forts
rain slaughtering destruction
and ruin, that will cast away their shields:
and for these citizens here
win glory and of the city
be the rescuers.

Then stand fair in your places                                         320
to receive our shrill prayers.

Pity it were that this city, so ancient,
should be cast to the House of Death,
a spear-booty, a slave,
in crumbling ashes, dishonorably,
sacked by an Achaean, with the Gods' consent;
that its women be haled away,
captives, young and old,
dragged by the hair, as horses by the mane,
and their raiment torn about them.
Emptied the city wails                                                 330
as the captive spoil, with mingled cries,
is led to its doom.
This heavy fate is what I fear.
It is a woeful thing for maidens unripe,
before the marriage rites, to tread
this bitter journey from their homes.
I would say that the dead
are better off than this.
Alas, unlucky indeed the fate
of a city captured—                                                    340
murder, fire, and rapine,
all the city polluted by smoke,
and the breath of Ares on it
maddened, desecrating piety, slaying the people.

There is tumult through the town.
Against her comes a towering net.
Man stands against man with the spear and is killed.
Young mothers, blood-boltered,
cry bitterly for the babes at their breast.                            350
The roving bands of pillagers are all brothers;
he that has plunder meets with another;
he that is empty calls him that is empty,
wishing to have a partner, eager for a share

neither less nor yet equal.
From such things what shall one augur?

All sorts of grain fallen
strewn on the ground vex,
embitter the eye of the housewife.
The great, profuse gifts of the earth                    360
in reckless streams of waste are poured out.
The girls, new servants, new to misery,
must endure a war captive's bed,
bed of a man successful.
Theirs the expectation of night's consummation
but for a triumphant enemy
to help their tearful sorrow.

*Half-Chorus*

Here, I think, friends, your scout comes bringing
some news of the enemy—hastily urging                    370
the joints of his legs to carry him here.

*Half-Chorus*

And here is the king himself, the son
of Oedipus in the nick of time to hear
the messenger's story. He too is in haste
and nimbly steps along.

*Messenger*

                          I can declare—
I know it well—the enemy's position:
how each at the gates has won by lot his station.
At the Proetid gate Tydeus now thunders
but dares not cross Ismenus' ford; the prophet
forbids. The sacrifices are unfavorable.
Tydeus, enraged and thirsting for the fight,               380
threatens, like serpents' hiss at noonday;
strikes with abuse the wise seer, Oecleides,
"battle and death make him cringe

118

through cowardice"—so he shouts aloud
and shakes his threefold shadowing plumes,
mane of his crested helm. Beneath his shield,
inside, ring brazen bells, a peal of terror,
and on the shield he bears this arrogant
device—a fashioned sky afire with stars.
In the shield's midst a glorious full moon,
night's eye, the eldest of the stars, stands out.          390
With such mad bragging and with overweening
trappings of war he roars along the banks
in love with battle, like the horse that chafes
against the bit, high mettled, impatient, hearing
the trumpet's sound. Against this champion
whom will you set?
When the bolts are shot back at the Proetid gates,
who will be champion fit to deserve our trust?

*Eteocles*

No equipment of a man will make me tremble
Devices on a shield deal no one wounds.
The plumes and bells bite not without the spear.
And for this night you speak of on his shield          400
glistening with all the stars of heaven—someone
may find his folly prophetic to himself.
For if in death night fall upon his eyes,
to him that bears this pompous blazonry
it shall be truly and most justly pregnant,
and he shall make his insolence prophesy
against himself.
                    I nominate against him
as champion of these gates to challenge Tydeus,
the worthy son of Astacus—right noble,
one honoring the throne of Modesty
and hating insolent words.                               410
Laggard in all things base he is wont to be
but not a coward. From those sown men
whom Ares spared his root springs—very native

is Melanippus to this land. His deeds
shall Ares with his dice determine;
but Justice, blood of his blood, sends him **forth,**
surely, to turn the enemy's spear away
from the mother that has borne him.

*Chorus*

May the Gods grant
good luck to our champion,
since justly he comes forward
a fighter for us.
But I fear for our friends                                    420
to look upon bloodshed
of those we love, dying.

*Messenger*

Yes, may the Gods grant him good luck.
At Electra's gates stands by lot Capaneus,
a giant this man, taller than the other,
and his threats breathe inhuman arrogance.
Our towers he menaces with terrors—Fortune
fulfil them not!—for he declares he'll sack
our city with the Gods' good will or ill.
Not even Zeus's wrath striking the earth
before him shall be obstacle to his purpose.
The lightnings and the thunderbolts he likened        430
to the sun's warm rays at noontide.
His device a naked man that carries fire,
in his hands, ablaze, a torch all ready. In gold
are letters that declare "I'll burn the city."
Against this man send—who will meet him?
Who will abide his threats and never tremble?

*Eteocles*

This man's boasts, too, beget us other gain.
For of the haughtiness of vain men, true
accuser proves their own tongue. Capaneus

threatens to do—and is prepared to do— 440
disdains the Gods, and giving exercise
to his mouth, in vain joy, up to heaven
mortal though he is, against Zeus sends his words,
shouted in swelling pride. I trust on him
will justly come the bolt that carries fire
in no way like the sun's warm rays at noontide.
Against him, be his lips never so insolent,
a man of fiery spirit shall be stationed,
strong Polyphontes, a guard trustworthy,
by favor of protecting Artemis
and of the other Gods. Tell me another 450
that has his place by lot at another gate.


*Chorus*

Destruction on him that against the city
vaunts huge threats;
may the thunderbolt's blast restrain him
before he burst into my house,
before he ravish me from my maiden room.


*Messenger*

Now I shall tell him that by lot won next
station at the gates. The third lot cast
jumped from the upturned brazen helmet
in favor of a third man, Eteoclus,
that he should lead his regiment in a charge 460
against the gates of Neïs. He wheels his mares
snorting in their nose bands, ready to charge the gate.
Pipes on the bridle bands filled with insolent
nostril breath whistle in a foreign note.
His shield, too, has its design—and that no lowly—
a man in armor mounts a ladder's steps
to the enemy's town to sack it. Loud
cries also this man in his written legend
"Ares himself shall not cast me from the tower."

Against him send some champion trustworthy 470
to turn the yoke of slavery from this city.

*Eteocles*
This man I'll send and may good luck go with him!

There, he is gone. His boast is in his hands
Megareus, Creon's son, and of the seed
and race of the sown men. He will not blench
at the furious neighing of horses nor yield the gates.
Either by death he'll pay his nurture's due
to his own land or he will capture two men
and city as depicted on the shield
and crown his father's house with the spoils of war.
On with another's boasts—don't grudge me the story. 480

*Chorus*
Good success to you, I pray,
Champion of my house,
and to the enemy ill success!
as with wild extravagance
they prate against the city
with maddened heart, so may Zeus
the Avenger look on them in wrath.

*Messenger*
Another, the fourth, holds the gate that neighbors
Onca Athena, and takes his station with a shout,
Hippomedon's vast frame and giant form.
He whirled a disc around—I mean the circle
of his shield—until I shuddered. I speak truth. 490
The armorer cannot have been a poor one
that put upon the shield this work of art—
a Typho hurling from his fiery mouth
black smoke, the flickering sister of fire.
The rim that ran around the hollow boss

of the shield is solid wrought with coiling snakes.
The man himself cried out his warcry, he,
inspired by Ares, revels in violence
like a Bacchanal with murder in his glance.
Take good heed how you deal with such a man;
he boasts even now at the gate he will raise panic.                    500

*Eteocles*

First Onca Pallas, with her place beside
our city, neighbor to our gates, will hate
the fellow's violence and keep him off,
as it were a chill snake from her nestling brood.
And then Hyperbius, the stout son of Oenops,
has been chosen to match him man for man, right willing,
at fortune's need, to put his fate to question—
no man to be reproached either in form
or spirit or in bearing of his arms.
Hermes has matched the two with excellent reason,
for man with man they shall engage as foes
and on their shields shall carry enemy Gods.                          510
The one has Typho breathing fire, the other,
Hyperbius, has father Zeus in station
sitting upon his shield, and in his hand
a burning bolt.
No one has yet seen Zeus defeated anywhere.
Such on each side are the favors of the Gods;
we are on the winning side, they with the vanquished
if Zeus than Typho mightier prove in battle.                         520

*Chorus*

Sure am I that he who hath
Zeus's foe upon his shield
the unloved form of the earth-born God,
the likeness hated by men
and the long-living Gods,
shall lay his head before our gates.

*Messenger*

 So may it prove. Now I shall take the fifth
 that has his station at the fifth, the Northern gate,
 right by Amphion's tomb that sprung from Zeus.
 By his lance he swears—and with sure confidence
 he holds it more in reverence than a god,   530
 more precious than his eyes—he will sack the town
 of Thebes in despite of Zeus. Such the loud vaunt
 of this creature sprung of a mountain mother, handsome,
 something between man and boy.
 The beard is newly sprouting on his cheeks,
 the thick, upspringing hair of youth in its bloom.
 His spirit unlike his maiden name* is savage,
 and with a grim regard he now advances.
 He too boasts high as he draws near our gates.
 For on his brazen shield, his body's rounded
 defense, he swings an insult to our city,   540
 the Sphinx that ate men raw, cunningly wrought,
 burnished, embossed, secured with rivets there.
 A man she bears beneath her, a Cadmaean,
 so that at him most of our darts shall fly.
 When he comes to the battle, so it seems,
 he will not play the petty shopkeeper
 nor shame the course of his long journey here—
 Parthenopaeus of Arcadia.
 He lives among our enemy presently
 and pays to Argos a fair wage for his keep,
 with threats against our forts—which God fulfil not.

*Eteocles*

 Would that they might obtain what from the Gods  550
 they pray against us—them, and their impious boasts.
 Then would they perish utterly and ill.
 We have a man to encounter your Arcadian,
 a man unboasting but his hand looks for
 the thing that should be done—Actor, the brother

 * Parthenopaeus: Maiden One.

of him I spoke of earlier. He will not suffer
a heedless tongue to flow within our gates
and to breed mischief, nor to cross our walls,
one bearing on an enemy shield the likeness
of the most hateful Sphinx—or else the beast
borne outside shall have cause of blame against                560
him that would carry her in, for many a hammering
blow she will get beneath the city's walls.
With the God's will, I may indeed speak truth.

*Chorus*

The words go through my heart;
the hair stands upright on my head;
as I listen to mighty words
of impious boasting men.
May the Gods destroy them within our land!

*Messenger*

A sixth I'll tell you of—a most modest man
greatest in might of battle, yet a prophet,
strong Amphiaraus, at the Homoloian gates                570
stationed, shouts insults at strong Tydeus: "Murderer,
cause of confusion to the city, greatest
teacher of evil to Argos; of the Fury
a summoning herald; servant of bloodshed;
adviser to Adrastus of all these evils."
And then again with eyes uplifted calling
on your own brother, strong prince Polyneices,
he dwells twice on the latter part of his name.*
And this is the speech to which his lips give utterance:
"Is such a deed as this dear to the Gods,                580
and fair to hear and tell of, for posterity,
for one to sack his native city, destroy
the gods of his country, bringing in
an alien enemy host?
                    What justice
* The latter half of the Greek word Polyneices means "strife."

125

shall quench the spring of guilt of another murder?
Your fatherland destroyed by the spear
which your own zeal impelled—shall it be your ally?
But for myself I shall make fat this soil
a prophet buried under enemy ground.
Let us fight. The fate I look for is right honorable."
So spoke the prophet brandishing his round          590
brazen shield. No device is on its circle.
He is best not at seeming to be such
but being so. Deep indeed is the furrow
of his mind from which he gathers fruit, and good
the counsels that do spring from it. For him
send out, I recommend, wise and good challengers,
for he is dangerous who reveres the gods.

*Eteocles*

Alas, the luck which among human beings
conjoins an honest man with impious wretches!
In every enterprise is no greater evil
than bad companionship: there is no fruit          600
that can be gathered. The field of doom
bears death as its harvest.
Indeed, a pious man, going on board
as shipmate of a crew of rascal sailors
and of some mischief they have perpetrated,
has often died with the God-detested breed;
or a just man, with fellow citizens
themselves inhospitable, forgetful of the Gods,
has fallen into the same snare as the unrighteous,
and smitten by the common scourge of God
has yielded up his life.
                    Even so this seer,
this son of Oecles, wise, just, good, and holy,          610
a prophet mighty, mingling with the impious—
against his better reason—with loud-mouthed
men who pursue a road long to retrace,
with God's will shall be dragged to their general doom.

I think he will not even assault the gate—
not that he is a coward or faint of spirit—
but well he knows how he must die in the battle
if Loxias' prophecies shall bear fruit.
Loxias either says nothing or speaks seasonably.
Yet against him, the strong prince Lasthenes          620
we shall range in combat, an inhospitable
sentry, in mind an old man but a young one
in his body's vigor, in his swift-swooping charge,
in his hand, undelaying to snatch a spear
and hurl it against the unprotected shield side.
But success—that is for men the gift of God alone.

Chorus

Hear, O ye Gods, our lawful prayers
and bring them to fulfilment that
the city prosper, averting
the horrors of war upon our invaders.
May Zeus strike them and slay them
with his bolt outside of our walls.          630

Messenger

Lo, now, the seventh at the seventh gate
I shall unfold—your own, your very brother.
Hear how he curses the city and what fate
he invokes upon her. He prays that once his feet
are set upon her walls, once he is proclaimed
a conqueror of this land, once he has cried
paean of triumph in its overthrow,
he then may close in fight with you and killing
may find his death beside your corpse.
Or if you live, that he may banish you—
in the selfsame way as you dishonored him—
to exile. So he shouts and calls the Gods
of his race and of his fatherland to witness          640
his prayers—a very violent Polyneices.

He bears a new-made, rounded shield
and a twofold device contrived thereon:
a woman leading modestly a man
conducts him, pictured as a warrior,
wrought all in gold. She claims she is Justice,
and the inscription reads: I will bring him home
and he shall have his city and shall walk
in his ancestral house.
                              Such are the signs.
But you yourself determine whom to send.                 650
You shall not find a fault in my report:
but you determine how to steer the state.


*Eteocles*

Our race, our race, the race of Oedipus,
by the Gods maddened, by them greatly hated;
alas, my father's curses are now fulfilled!
But for me no crying and no lamentation
lest even sorer sorrow be begotten.
I tell you, Polyneices, so well named,
soon we shall know the pertinence of your sign,
whether your golden characters on the shield,            660
babbling, in wild distraction of the mind,
will indeed bring you home. This might have been,
if Justice, Zeus's virgin daughter had stood
by his actions and his mind. But in his flight
out of the darkness of his mother's womb,
in his growth as a child, in his young manhood,
in the first gathering of his chin's hair—no, never
did Justice look upon him nor regard him.
I do not think that now he comes to outrage
this fatherland of his she will stand his ally,
or else she is called falsely Justice, joining           670
with a man whose mind conceives no limit in villainy.
In this I trust and to the conflict with him
I'll go myself. What other has more right?
King against king, and brother against brother,

128

foe against foe we'll fight.
                              Bring me my greaves
to shield me from the lances and the stones.

*Chorus*

O dearest son of Oedipus, do not
be like in temper to this utterer
of dreadful sayings. There are enough Cadmaeans
to grapple with the Argives: such blood is expiable.          680
But for the blood of brothers mutually shed
there is no growing old of the pollution.

*Eteocles*

If a man suffer ill, let it be without shame;
this is the only gain when we are dead.
For deeds both evil and disgraceful never
will you say word of good.

*Chorus*

What do you long for, child?
Let not the frantic lust
for battle, filling the heart
carry you away. Expel
the evil passion at its birth.

*Eteocles*

It is the God that drives this matter on.
Since it is so—on, on with favoring wind          690
this wave of hell that has engulfed for its share
all kin of Laius, whom Phoebus has so hated.

*Chorus*

Bitter-biting indeed
is the passion that urges you
to accomplish manslaying,
bitter in fruit,
where the blood to be shed is unlawful.

*Eteocles*

> Yes, for the hateful black
> curse of my father loved
> sits on my dry and tearless eyes
> and tells me first of gain and then of death.

*Chorus*

> Resist its urging: coward
> you shall not be called
> if you rule your life well.
> Forth from your house the black-robed Fury                700
> shall go, when from your hands
> the Gods shall receive a sacrifice.

*Eteocles*

> We are already past the care of Gods.
> For them our death is the admirable offering.
> Why then delay, fawning upon our doom?

*Chorus*

> Not when the chance is yours—
> for in the veering change
> of spirit though late
> perhaps the God may change
> and come with kinder breath.
> Now his blast is full.

*Eteocles*

> The curse of Oedipus has fanned that blast.
> Too true the vision of sleepy nightmares                710
> showing division of my father's heritage.

*Chorus*

> Listen to women though you like it not.

*Eteocles*

> Speak then of what may be. Nor should it be long.

*Chorus*

Go not you, go not, to the seventh gate.

*Eteocles*

No words of yours will blunt my whetted purpose.

*Chorus*

Yet even bad victory the Gods hold in honor.

*Eteocles*

No soldier may endure to hear such words.

*Chorus*

Do you wish to reap as harvest a brother's blood?

*Eteocles*

If Gods give ill, no man may shun their giving.

*Chorus*

I shudder at the Goddess,                                     720
unlike all other Gods,
who compasses destruction of the house,
utterly unforgetting, prophet of ill,
the Fury invoked by a father's curse.
I dread that it bring to pass
the furious invocations
of Oedipus astray in his mind.
This strife, death to his sons, spurs it on.

A stranger grants them land-allotment,
a Chalyb, Scythian colonist,
a bitter divider of possessions—
iron-hearted Steel.                                          730
Yes, he has allotted them land to dwell in
as much as the dead may possess:
no share theirs of their broad acres.

When they die with mutual hand
mutually slaughtering
and earth's dust shall drink
black clotted murder-blood,
who shall then give purification,
who shall wash away the stain?
O new evils of the house,                                    740
new mingled with the old.

Old is the tale of sin I tell
but swift in retribution:
to the third generation it abides.
Thrice in Pythian prophecies
given at Navel-of-Earth
Apollo had directed
King Laius all issueless to die
and save his city so . . .

but he was mastered by loving folly                          750
and begot for himself a doom,
father-murdering Oedipus,
who sowed his mother's sacred womb,
whence he had sprung himself,
with bloody root, to his heartbreak.
Madness was the coupler
of this distracted pair.

Now, as it were, a sea
drives on the wave:
one sinks, another rises,                                    760
triple-crested around the prow
of the city, and breaks in foam.
Our defense between is but a little thing
no bigger than a wall in width.
I fear that with our princes
our city be subdued.

For heavy is the settlement
of ancient curses, to fulfilment brought.
That evil when fulfilled
passes not away.
Prosperity grown over fat
of men, gain seeking,                                    770
compels jettisoning
of all goods, utterly.

What man has earned such admiration
of Gods and men that shared his city
and of the general throng of mortal men,
as Oedipus—who ever had such honor
as he that from his land had banished
the Sphinx, that ate men up?

But when in misery he knew
the meaning of his dreadful marriage,
in pain distraught, in heart distracted             780
he brought a double sorrow to fulfilment.
With patricidal hand
he reft himself of eyes
that dearer to him were than his own children.
And on those children savage
maledictions he launched
for their cruel tendance of him
and wished they might divide
with iron-wielding hand his own possessions.
And now I fear                                           790
that nimble-footed Fury bring those wishes to fulfilment.

*Messenger*

Take heart, you mother's darlings, this your city
has escaped the yoke of slavery. Fallen
are the vauntings of the monstrous men.
Our city is in smooth water and though many
the assaults of the waves, has shipped no sea.

Our wall still stands protecting us, our gates
we barricaded with trustworthy champions.
For the most part all is well—at six of the gates.
The seventh the Lord Apollo, Captain of Sevens,*     800
took to himself: on Oedipus' race
he has fulfilled Laius' ancient follies.

*Chorus*

What new and evil thing concerns the city?

*Messenger*

The city is saved, but the twin princes—

*Chorus*

Who? What do you mean? Through fear of your words
    I am frantic.

*Messenger*

Get your wits and hear. Oedipus' two sons—

*Chorus*

Alas, alas, the ills I prophesied.

*Messenger*

In very truth, crushed to the ground.     810

*Chorus*

They lie there? Bitter though it be, yet speak.

*Messenger*

The men have fallen, one another's killers.

*Chorus*

Did brother's hands achieve a mutual murder?
* "Captain of Sevens" is an ancient cult title of Apollo.

*Messenger*
The ground has drunk the blood shed each by each.

*Chorus*
So all too equal was their guiding spirit.

*Messenger*
Surely he destroys this most unlucky race.
Here is store of sorrow and joy at once.
The city has good fortune, but its lords,
the two generals, have divided the possessions
with hammered steel of Scythia. They shall have
what land suffices for a grave, swept thither
down the wind of their father's ill-boding curses.          820

*Chorus*
O great Zeus and Spirits that guard
the city, you Protectors
that guard our walls:
shall I rejoice, shall I cry aloud
for our city's safety?
Or for those wretched ones, luckless and childless,
our generals, shall I lament?
They have earned their name too well
and "men of strife" they have perished          830
through impious intent.


O black curse consummated
on the race, the curse of Oedipus!
An evil chill assails my heart.
I raise the dirge at the tomb
like a Bacchanal, hearing
of their blood-dripping corpses,
of their ill-fated death.
Ill-omened indeed
is this melody of the Spear.

It has worked to an end, not failed,                    840
the curses called on them by their father of old.
The decisions of Laius, wanting in faith,
have had effect till now.
My heart is troubled for the city;
divine warnings are not blunted.
O full of sorrows, this you have done
a deed beyond belief.
Woes worthy of groaning
have come in very truth.


(*The bodies of the princes are carried in, escorted
by their two sisters, Ismene and Antigone.*)
Here is visible evidence of the messenger's tale.
Twofold our griefs and double
the ills these two men wrought;
double the fated sorrow
now brought to fulfilment.                              850
What shall I say but that
here sorrows, sorrows' children,
abide at the hearth of the house?
But, my friends, down the wind of groans
with hands that beat the head
ply the speeding stroke
which sends through Death's waters
the dark-sailed ship of mission
to the shore, untrodden by Apollo, and sunless,
the shore unseen, that welcomes all at last.           860
Here they come to their bitter task,
Ismene and Antigone,
to make the dirge for their brothers.
With true sincerity, I think,
from their deep bosoms,
they shall utter a song of grief that fits the cause.
Us it concerns to sing,
before their song,

the ill-sounding Furies' dirge,
and the hateful Hades paean. 870

O most luckless of all women
that fasten the girdle about their robes,
I cry, I groan: there is no guile
in my heart to check my true dirge.

*Antigone (speaking over the bodies)*
    O you misguided ones,
    faithless to friends, unwearied in evil,
    you who plundered your father's house
    to your misery, with the spear.

*Chorus*
    Wretched indeed those who wretched death
    have found to the ruin of their house. 880

*Ismene*
    O you that tore the roof
    from our house, you that glimpsed
    the bitter sovereignty, at last
    you are reconciled—by the sword.

*Chorus*
    Too truly has that dread spirit,
    the Fury of Oedipus,
    brought all this to fulfilment.

*Antigone*
    Stricken through the left sides
    stricken indeed,
    through sides born of a common mother. 890
    Alas, strange ones,
    alas for the curse
    of death that answered death!

137

*Chorus*

A straight thrust to house and body
delivered by unspeakable wrath,
by the doom invoked by a father's curse,
which they shared without discord.

*Ismene*

Through the city the cry of weeping;
the walls groan aloud;                                        900
the plain that loved them groans aloud.
There abide for their descendants
the possessions for which
their bitter fate was paid,
for which their strife arose,
for which they found the end of death.

*Chorus*

In bitterness of heart they shared
their possessions in equality:
no blame from friends
has their arbitrator,
Ares, impartial to both sides.                               910

*Antigone*

By the stroke of the sword they are as they are
by the stroke of the sword there awaits them—what?
The share in their ancestral tomb, says someone.

*Chorus*

A shrill cry escorts them from their house,
a cry heartrending,
a cry for its own griefs, its own woes,
in anguish of mind with no thought of joy,              920
weeping tears from a heart that breaks,
for these our two princes.

138

*Ismene*

    One may say over the bodies
    of this unhappy pair:
    much they have done to their fellow citizens,
    and much to all the ranks of foreigners
    who died in this destructive war.

*Chorus*

    Unlucky she that bore them
    above all womankind
    that are called by a mother's name.
    She took as husband her own child
    and bore these who have died              930
    their brotherly hands working each other's murder.

*Antigone*

    Brotherly indeed in utter destruction
    in unkindly severance,
    in frantic strife,
    in the ending of their quarrel.

*Chorus*

    Their enmity is ended, in the earth
    blood-drenched their life is mingled.
    Very brothers are they now.             940
    Bitter the reconciler of their feud,
    stranger from over the sea,
    sped hither by the fire,
    whetted steel.
    A bitter and evil divider of possessions,
    Ares, who made their father's curse
    a thing of utter truth.

*Ismene*

    They have their share, unhappy ones
    of Zeus given sorrows:

beneath their bodies, earth
in fathomless wealth shall lie.                                    950

*Chorus* (*speaking over the bodies*)
You who have made your race
blossom with many woes:
over you at last have cried
the Curses their shrill lament,
and the race is turned to confusion and rout.
The trophy of Destruction stands
at the gates where they were smitten
and conqueror of the two
the Spirit at last has come to rest.                              960

(*The dirge proper. The sisters stand each at the head
of one of the corpses.*)

*Antigone*
You smote and were smitten.

*Ismene*
You killed and were slain.

*Antigone*
By the spear you killed.

*Ismene*
By the spear you died.

*Antigone*
Wretched in acting.

*Ismene*
Wretched in suffering.

*Antigone*
Let the groans go forth.

*Ismene*
Let the tears fall.

*Antigone*
You lie in death—

*Ismene*
having killed—

*Antigone and Ismene*
Woe, woe.

*Antigone*
My mind is distraught with groans.

*Ismene*
With groans my heart is full.

*Antigone*
Alas, alas, creature of tears.

*Ismene*
Alas, again, all-miserable.                    970

*Antigone*
By a loving hand you died.

*Ismene*
And killed one that loved you.

*Antigone*
A double sorrow to relate.

*Ismene*
A double sorrow to see.

*Antigone*
Two sorrows hard by one another.

*Ismene*
Brother's sorrow close to brother's.

*Chorus*
O wretched Fate, giver of heaviness,
awful shade of Oedipus,
black Fury,
verily a spirit mighty in strength!

*Ismene and Antigone*
Woe, woe.

*Antigone*
Evils unfit to look upon—

*Ismene*
have you shown after banishment.

*Antigone*
He came not back when he had slain.          980

*Ismene*
This one saved, lost his own life.

*Antigone*
This one died—

*Ismene*
and killed the other.

*Antigone*
Race unhappy.

*Ismene*
Deed unhappy.

*Antigone*
Grievous sorrows of kindred.

*Ismene*
  Grievous, thrice grievous sorrow.

*Chorus*
  O wretched Fate, giver of heaviness,
  awful shade of Oedipus,
  black Fury,
  verily a spirit mighty in strength.

*Antigone*
  You have learned the lesson by experience.

*Ismene*
  And you have learned it, no whit later.                990

*Antigone*
  When you returned to the city—

*Ismene*
  yes, to face him with your spear.

*Antigone*
  Deadly to tell.

*Ismene*
  Deadly to see.

*Antigone*
  Pain—

*Ismene*
  ill—

*Antigone*
  to house and land—

*Ismene*
  and most of all to me.

*Antigone*
O unhappy king of sorrow!

*Ismene*
O of all most rich in pain!                                  1000

*Antigone*
Where shall we lay them in the earth?

*Ismene*
Where their honor is greatest.

*Antigone*
O brothers possessed by evil spirits, in doom—

*Ismene*
that will sleep by the side of their father to his hurt.

*Herald*
It is my duty to declare to you,
counselors of the people, the resolves
already taken and the present pleasure
of this Cadmaean city. . . .
Our Lord Eteocles for his loyalty
it is determined to bury in the earth
that he so loved. Fighting its enemies
he found his death here. In the sight
of his ancestral shrines he is pure and blameless        1010
and died where young men die right honorably.
These are my instructions to communicate
with respect to him. His brother Polyneices,
or rather his dead body, you must cast out
unburied, for the dogs to drag and tear
as fits one who would have destroyed our country
had not some God proved obstacle to his spear.
Even in death he shall retain this guilt
against his Gods ancestral whom he dishonored

144

when he brought his foreign host here for invasion
and would have sacked the city. So it is resolved
that he shall have, as his penalty, a burial   1020
granted dishonorably by the birds of the air
and that no raising of a mound by hand
attend him nor observance of keening dirge.
Unhonored shall his funeral be by friends.
This is the pleasure of the Cadmaean state.

*Antigone*
So I to the Cadmaean magistrates
declare: if no one else will dare to join me
in burying him, yet will I bury him
and take the danger on my head alone
when that is done. He is my brother. I
am not ashamed of this anarchic act   1030
of disobedience to the city. Strange,
a strange thing is the common blood we spring from—
a mother wretched, a father doomed to evil.
Willingly then with one that would not will it,
live spirit with dead man in sisterhood
I shall bear my share. His flesh
the hollow-bellied wolves shall never taste of.
Let that be no one's "pleasure or decree."
His tomb and burying place I will contrive
though but a woman. In the bosom folds
of my linen robe I shall carry earth to him.
And I shall cover him: let no one determine
the contrary. Be of good cheer (*to her sister*), I shall  1040
find means to bring my will to pass.

*Herald*
       I forbid
this act, defiance of the city's pleasure.

*Antigone*
I forbid you your superfluous proclamations.

145

*Herald*
> Harsh is the people now that danger's past.

*Antigone*
> Harsh truly. But *he* shall not go unburied.

*Herald*
> Him the state hates, will you grace with a tomb?

*Antigone*
> Long since the Gods determined of his honor.

*Herald*
> Not till he cast in peril this land of ours.

*Antigone*
> He suffered ill and gave back what he suffered.

*Herald*
> This deed of his was aimed at all, not one.          1050

*Antigone*
> Last of the Gods Contention ends her tale.
> But I shall bury him: spare me long speech.

*Herald*
> Have your own way: but I forbid the act.

*Chorus*
> Alas, alas.
> O high-vaunting, ruin to the race
> fatal Furies, who have destroyed
> the race of Oedipus so utterly—
> What will happen me? What shall I do?
> What shall I plan?
> How shall I be so heartless,
> not to mourn for you,

not to give escort to your funeral?
But I fear the dreadful authority                    1060
of the people: I am turned from my purpose.

(*To the body of Eteocles*)
   Many mourners you shall win:

(*To the body of Polyneices*)
   But this poor wretch unwept
   save for his sister's single dirge
   shall go his road. Who would yield
   so much obedience as this?

                    (*The Chorus divides in two.*)

*First Half-Chorus*
   Let the state do or not
   what it will to the mourners of Polyneices.
   We will go and bury him;
   we will go as his escort.
   This grief is common to the race              1070
   but now one way and now another
   the city approves the path of justice.

*Second Half-Chorus*
   But we will go with the other, as the city
   and Justice jointly approve.
   For after the Blessed Ones and the strength of Zeus
   he is the one who saved the city
   from utter destruction, from being overwhelmed
   by the wave of foreign invaders.

# MODERN LIBRARY GIANTS

*A series of sturdily bound and handsomely printed, full-sized library editions of books formerly available only in expensive sets. These volumes contain from 600 to 1,400 pages each.*

**THE** MODERN LIBRARY GIANTS REPRESENT A SELECTION OF THE WORLD'S GREATEST BOOKS

## MISCELLANEOUS